P9-CMF-833

CHRISTUS CONSUMMATOR.

CHRISTUS CONSUMMATOR:

SOME ASPECTS OF THE WORK AND
PERSON OF CHRIST IN RELATION
TO MODERN THOUGHT.

BY

BROOKE FOSS WESTCOTT, D.D., D.C.L.,

CANON OF WESTMINSTER AND REGIUS PROFESSOR
OF DIVINITY, CAMBRIDGE.

SECOND EDITION.

London:

MACMILLAN AND CO.

AND NEW YORK

1887

αὕτη ἐcτὶν ἡ αἰώνιοc ζωὴ ἵνα γινώcκωcι cὲ τὸν
μόνον ἀληθινὸν θεόν, καὶ ὃν ἀπέcτειλαc Ἰηcοῦν
Χριcτόν.

ST JOHN XVII. 3.

FIRST EDITION PRINTED BY C. J. CLAY, M.A. & SONS, JULY, 1886.

PREFACE.

THE Sermons in the present volume, with the exception of the last, were preached in Westminster Abbey during my residence in *August* 1885 and *January* 1886. I have endeavoured in them to guide others to lines of thought which I have myself found to lead to that sure hope which we can reach *through patience and through comfort of the Scriptures.* I have added as an Appendix a Sermon preached at Cambridge, which was designed to give a practical application of this teaching.

The broad lessons of the Epistle to the Hebrews appear to me to shew how much that seems to be loss in regard to our religious circumstances proves to be gain by turning our minds from things temporal and provisional to Christ Himself. I sought therefore first to indicate these in a general outline, and then afterwards to point out a little more in detail some special aspects of the Person and Work of Christ which correspond with the wants of our own position.

The delays, the failures, the sorrows which beset the great life of humanity can be borne gladly if we are allowed even from afar to recognise the Presence of CHRISTUS CONSUMMATOR. The things of time are transfigured in the light of eternity.

The last words of the Founder of the Abbey express with pathetic force one side of the Truth. 'Weep not,' he said to the Queen sobbing by his side, 'Weep not my daughter. For I shall not die but live; and as I leave the land of the dying, I trust to see the blessings of the Lord in the land of the living.' The vision of that unchanging order is given to us even here in the Gospel. *Father...*, the Lord said of His disciples, *This is the life eternal, that they know Thee the only true GOD, and Him Whom Thou didst send, even Jesus Christ.*

B. F. W.

DIVINITY SCHOOL,
CAMBRIDGE.
May 24th, 1886.

NOTICE TO THE SECOND EDITION.

IN this Edition I have corrected one or two misprints, altered a few words, and endeavoured to make the sense of some passages more clear by a fuller punctuation. In other respects the Book is unchanged.

I cannot but add that the wide welcome which the Book has received has been to me a cause of great thankfulness. The thoughts which I have myself found helpful have proved—it has been my joy to learn—helpful to many others. Some indeed seem to have wholly misunderstood my purpose and meaning. But this was not surprising; for they had evidently not felt the difficulties which I sought to meet. Happy are they who have not felt them; but happier, I think, are they who, feeling them, are led, by a discipline which is at first painful, to a wider, deeper, fuller view of Him *in Whom are all the treasures of wisdom and knowledge, hidden*—hidden in order that they may be revealed in due season according to the needs of men.

B. F. W.

DIVINITY SCHOOL,
  CAMBRIDGE.
March 30th, 1887.

CHRISTUS CONSUMMATOR.

I.

LESSONS FROM AN EPOCH OF CHANGE.

I. *The trials of a new age.*

II. *The destiny of man fulfilled by Christ through suffering.*

x

Contents.

III. *The King Priest.*

IV. *The Universal Society.*

V. *The New Covenant.*

II.

ASPECTS OF THE INCARNATION.

I.   *The Incarnation a subject for devout study.*

II. *The Incarnation and the Creation.*

III. *The Incarnation and the Fall.*

APPENDIX.

The vision of GOD the call of the Prophet.

CHRISTUS CONSUMMATOR. I.

LESSONS FROM AN EPOCH OF CHANGE.

This word, Yet once more, signifieth the removing of those things that are shaken, as of things that have been made, that those things which are not shaken may remain.

HEBR. xii. 27.

THE TRIALS OF A NEW AGE.

EVERY age which is moved by the Spirit of I.
GOD feels keenly the searching, chastening
power of that Divine Presence. "He that is near Didym.
Me," the Lord is reported to have said, "is near *in Ps.*
lxxxviii. 8.
fire." And we cannot hope to enjoy the splendour
of a fuller, purer light without enduring the pain
which necessarily comes from the removal of the
veils by which it was obscured. Gain
through apparent loss; victory through moment-
ary defeat; the energy of a new life through John xvi.
pangs of travail; such has ever been the law of 21 f.
spiritual progress. This law has been fulfilled in
every crisis of reformation; and it is illustrated
for our learning in every page of the New Testament.

But in no apostolic writing is the truth un-
folded with such pathetic force as in the Epistle
to the Hebrews. And so it is, I think, that that
mysterious "word of consolation" appeals to us Hebr. xiii.
with a voice of thrilling power in our time of 22.

1—2

I.   trial, when the law of progress, the law of fruit-
fulness through death, seems to be hastening to a
fresh fulfilment.   The student of that
Epistle cannot but observe that no men were
ever called upon to endure greater sacrifices, to
surrender more precious hopes, to bear deeper
disappointments, than those to whom it was
first addressed.   Men who had lived in the light
of the Old Testament, men who had known the
joy of a noble ritual, men who had habitually
drawn near to GOD in intelligible ways, men who
had but lately welcomed Him in Whom they
believed that the glory of Israel should be con-
summated, were most unexpectedly required to
face what seemed to them to be the forfeiture of
all that they held dearest.   The letter of
Scripture, the worship of the temple, the expect-
ations of national triumph, had to be abandoned.
The heirs of the patriarchs, when they first felt
that they were entering on their inheritance,
were compelled, if they remained Christians, to
accept the position of outcasts from the ancient
commonwealth of GOD, and to confess themselves
followers of One crucified and rejected, Who
delayed to assume His throne.

And what then? They could not but begin
to reckon up their loss and gain. The fresh
Hebr. x.
32 ff.   enthusiasm of their early faith had died away in

the weary waiting of a lifetime. They had in
part degenerated because they had not grown.
But they were not uncared for in the crisis of
their peril. Out of the darkness of the gathering
storm, in which the Holy Place was to be for ever
swept away, came a voice which interpreted the
sad riddles of their fate. Under the
guidance of a nameless apostle, the Hebrews were
enabled to see how the sufferings of Christ were
not a difficulty in the way of His Messiahship, to
be compensated by a visible triumph, but the
very pledge of the fulfilment of the destiny of
man in spite of sin; to see how the unbelief of
Israel opened the way for the larger unfolding of
the world-wide counsels of GOD; to see how in
giving up type and shadow they secured the realities which these signified; to see how things
visible and transitory were replaced by things
unseen and eternal; to see how above the vanishing grace of the Levitical service rose in supreme
and sovereign majesty the figure of the ascended
Christ, Priest and King for ever, seated at the
right hand of GOD, infinite in sympathy and
power.

Now when we read the apostolic words, and
picture to ourselves the sorrows which they
illuminated—when we feel that in the portraiture
of the perils of early believers we have the record

1.
Hebr. vi.
11.

of true human struggles, and know that the essential elements of human discipline must always be the same—we cannot, I think, fail to recognise in the trials of the Hebrews of the first age an image of the peculiar trials by which we are beset; and so by their experience we may gain the assurance that for us also there is the promise of larger wisdom, where they found it, in Hebr. xii. 27. wider views of Christ's Person and Work, that *the removal of those things that are shaken* is brought about in order *that those things which are not shaken may remain* in serener and simpler beauty.

If we look at the circumstances of the Hebrews a little more closely we shall notice that the severity of their trials came in a great degree from mistaken devoutness. They had determined, in obedience to traditional opinion, what Scripture should mean; and they found it hard to enter into its wider teaching. They had determined that institutions which were of Divine appointment must be permanent; and they found it hard to grasp the realities by which the forms of the older worship were replaced. They had determined that Christ's sovereignty should be openly vindicated by the victorious faith of GOD's people; and they found it hard to hold their belief firm against the general unbelief of their fellow-countrymen.

Now in these respects, we cannot, as I said, fail to recognise that the difficulties of the Hebrews correspond with our own. For I am speaking now of the difficulties of those who hold to their first faith, and are yet conscious of shakings, changes, losses, of the removing of much which they formerly identified with it.   Many among us, for example, tremble with a vague fear when they find that that "Divine Library," in the noble language of Jerome, which we call the Bible—"the Books"— "the Book"—cannot be summarily separated by a sharp, unquestionable line from the other literature with which it is connected; that the text and the interpretation of the constituent parts have not been kept free from corruptions and ambiguities which require the closest exercise of critical skill; that deductions have been habitually drawn from incidental modes of expression in Scripture which cannot be maintained in the light of that fuller knowledge of GOD's working which He has given us.

Others again find the historical problems raised by the study of the Bible carried into a wider region. They learn in the turmoil of action, and they learn in the silence of their own souls, that the Faith can no longer be isolated and fenced off from rude questionings as something

I.   separate from common life. They perceive that
they must bear, as they can, to see the deepest
foundations of truth laid open and tested by impetuous inquirers; bear, as they can, to acknowledge once and again that formulas which, in
earlier times, seemed to declare the Gospel adequately, no longer cover the facts of the world as
they have been revealed to us in these later days.

And others have a more grievous trial still.
As their view of the world is widened; as they
come to understand better the capacities of
humanity and the claims of Christ; as they are
driven to compare the promises of the kingdom of
GOD with the present fruits of its sway; as they
feel that they cannot separate themselves from
the race of which they are heirs; as they look
upon the light, still after eighteen centuries
John i. 5. struggling (as it appears) against eclipse, their
heart may well sink within them. We cannot
wonder if such are tempted to ask with those of
2 Pet. iii. old times, *Where is the promise of His coming?*
4.   or to listen with little more than the sad protest
of a lonely trust to the bold assertions of those
who say that the Faith has exhausted its power in
dealing with the facts of an earlier and simpler
civilisation.

There is not, I believe, one who reads these
words—not one who looks with calm, open eyes

upon the spectacle of the world and the nearer
vision of his own nature—who has not been stirred
by the anxious thoughts which I have indicated,
and asked how they shall be met, met not by a
strong effort of overmastering will, but with that
quiet confidence which is able to welcome every
lesson of the discipline of GOD. And what then
shall we say? How shall we escape the double
danger which besets us, of hastily surrendering
every position which is boldly challenged, or of
rigidly refusing to consider arguments which tend
to modify traditional opinion?

I do not doubt for one moment as to my
answer. I bid those who are tempted to accept
their trials with the frankest trust, as the conditions through which they will be brought to
know GOD better. I have been forced by
the peculiar circumstances of my work to regard
from many sides the difficulties which beset our
historic Faith. If I know by experience their
significance and their gravity; if I readily allow
that on many points I wish for fuller light; then
I claim to be heard, when I say without reserve
that I have found each region of anxious trial
fruitful in blessing: that I have found my devout
reverence for every word of the Bible quickened
and deepened, when I have acknowledged that it
demands the exercise of every faculty with which

I. I have been endowed, and, that as it touches the life of man at every point, it welcomes, for its fuller understanding, the help which comes from every gain of human knowledge : that I have found my absolute trust in the Gospel of the Word Incarnate confirmed with living power, when I have seen with growing clearness that no phrases of the schools can adequately express its substance, or do more than help men provisionally to realise some part of its relation to thought and action ; when I have learnt through the researches of students in other fields to extend the famous words of the Roman dramatist, and say " *Christianus sum : nihil in rerum natura a me alienum puto* "—" I am a Christian ; and therefore nothing in man and nothing in nature can fail to command the devotion of my reverent study"— : that I have found, even in the slow and fitful progress of the Church, which still does move forward, a spring of hope, when I turn, as I must turn from time to time, to take count of the unutterable evils of great cities, and great nations, and whole continents, which wait for atonement and redemption in the longsuffering and wisdom of GOD. Yes, if, as I have endeavoured to shew, our trials, the trials of a new age, correspond with those of the Hebrews, the consolation which availed for them, avails for us also. We shall find

in due course, as they found, that all we are
required to surrender—child-like prepossessions,
venerable types of opinion, partial and impatient
hopes—is given back to us in a new revelation of
Christ; that He is being brought nearer to us,
and shewn in fresh glory, through the "fallings
from us, vanishings of sense and earthly things"
which we had been inclined to identify with
Himself.

There is a picture with which we are all
familiar, in which Christ seated in glory is represented as dispensing His gifts to the representa-
tives of suffering humanity.   From His hands the
slave receives freedom and the sick health : the
mourner finds rest in His sympathy, old men
peace, children joy.   *"Christus Consolator"* is
indeed an image which touches every heart.   But
it is not the whole Gospel.   It is not, I venture to
think, the particular aspect of the Gospel which is
offered by the Spirit of GOD to us now for our
acknowledgment.   Sin, suffering, sorrow, are not
the ultimate facts of life.   These are the work of
an enemy; and the work of our GOD and Saviour
lies deeper.   The Creation stands behind Gen. i. 27.
the Fall, the counsel of the Father's love behind
the self-assertion of man's wilfulness.   And I
believe that if we are to do our work we must
learn to think, not only of the redemption of man

I.

but also of the accomplishment of the Divine
purpose for all that GOD made. We must learn to

Eph. i. 10. think of that *summing up of all things in Christ,*
in the phrase of St Paul, which crowns the last
aspirations of physicist and historian with a final
benediction. We must dare, in other words, to
look beyond Christ the Consoler to Christ the
Fulfiller. *Christus Consolator*—let us thank GOD
for the revelation which leaves no trial of man
unnoticed and unsoothed—leads us to *Christus
Consummator*.

This thought of "Christ the Fulfiller" is, as it
seems to me, the characteristic teaching of the
Epistle to the Hebrews. The author of that
marvellous book, speaking to the heart with a
pathos to which the prophecy of Jeremiah offers
the only parallel in the Bible, shews us in many
ways how He through whom GOD made the world
in all the rich variety of its growing life, has been

c. i. 2.   appointed heir of all things; how He has fulfilled
c. ii. 9.   the destiny of men in spite of the inroad of sin,
and borne humanity to the throne of the Father;

cc. iv. 14 ff.; how in the plenitude of royal majesty He appears
ix. 24.   before GOD for those whose nature He has taken

cc. x. 19;   to Himself; how in Him we have present access
xii. 22 ff. to a spiritual society, in which earth and heaven,
men and angels, are united in a glorious fellowship; how He has given us for our daily support

a covenant and a service, which transfigure the conditions of our conflict into sacraments of a higher order.

I.
cc. viii. 6;
xiii. 10.

These, then, are the four thoughts which I wish to follow out in due succession. They meet our difficulties, as far as I can judge, with messages of widened hope, as they met the difficulties of the Hebrews. They enable us to realise with a personal and present conviction, that the Spirit of GOD is even now *taking of the things of Christ, and shewing them unto us ;* that we too are living in an age of revelation, and called to listen to a Divine voice.

John xvi.
14.

And if the thoughts seem strange to any, and removed from the familiar circle of religious reflection ; if they require devout patience for their mastering ; if they add an element of infinite interest to the commonest details of life, and therefore claim the tribute of complete self-surrender ; let us remember that progress is still, as in the first age, the essence of our faith. We have to gather little by little the fruits of a victory in which Christ has overcome the world. The Hebrews were, as we have seen, in danger of apostasy, because they failed to go forward. And that we may be shielded from the like peril, the words which were spoken to them are spoken also to us : *let us be borne on to*

John xvi.
33.

Hebr. vi. 1.

I.   *perfection,* not simply " let us go on," or even " let us press on," as if the advance depended on the vigour of our own effort, but " let us be borne on," " borne on " with that mighty influence which waits only for the acceptance of faith, that it may exert its sovereign sway, " borne on " by Him whose unseen arms are outstretched beneath the most weary and the weakest, " borne on " by Him who is the Way and the End of all human endeavour.

And as we are thus " borne on," as we yield ourselves, yield every gift of mind and body, of place and circumstance, yield all that we cherish most tenderly, to the service of Him in Whom we are made more than conquerors, let us not fear that we shall lose the sense of the vastness of the Divine life in our glad consciousness of its immediate power.   We assuredly shall not fail in reverent gratitude to our fathers for the inheritance which they have bequeathed to us, while we acknowledge that it is our duty to improve it.   We shall not disparage the past, while we accept the inspiring responsibility of using to the uttermost the opportunities of the present.   We shall cling with the simplest devotion to every article of our ancient Creed, while we believe, and act as believing, that *this is eternal life, that we may know*—know, as the

Rom. viii. 37.

John xvii. 3 ; 1 John v. 20.

original word implies, with a knowledge which is extended from generation to generation, and from day to day,—*the only true GOD and Jesus Christ.*

By the pursuit of this knowledge we come to recognise that the difficulties which press us most sorely are really the discipline through which GOD is teaching us: veiled promises of coming wisdom. We learn through the living lessons of our own experience that the eternal Gospel covers the facts of life, its sorrows, its needs, its joys, its wealth. Through every conflict the Truth is seen in the majesty of its growing vigour. Shakings, shakings not of the earth only but of the heaven, will come; but what then? We know this, that all that falls is taken away *that those things which are not shaken may remain.*

II.

THE DESTINY OF MAN FULFILLED BY CHRIST THROUGH SUFFERING.

Not unto angels did he subject the world to come, whereof we speak. But one hath somewhere testified, saying, What is man, that thou art mindful of him? Or the son of man, that thou visitest him? Thou madest him a little lower than the angels; thou crownedst him with glory and honour, and didst set him over the works of thy hands: thou didst put all things in subjection under his feet. For in that he subjected all things unto him, he left nothing that is not subject to him. But now we see not yet all things subjected to him. But we behold him who hath been made a little lower than the angels, even Jesus, because of the suffering of death crowned with glory and honour, that by the grace of God he should taste death for every man. For it became him, for whom are all things, and through whom are all things, in bringing many sons unto glory, to make the author of their salvation perfect through sufferings.

HEBR. ii. 5—10.

THE DESTINY OF MAN FULFILLED BY
CHRIST THROUGH SUFFERING.

THE form of the Epistle to the Hebrews is II.
unique among the writings of the New Testament.   Without preface and without salutation
the Apostolic author opens the innermost treasury
of GOD, and *brings out things new and old*.   He Matt. xiii.
boldly re-affirms, with abrupt and majestic elo- 52.
quence, the glory of the Christian Faith, by disclosing a fuller prospect of the person and the
work of Christ.   He shews how the manifold Hebr. i.
lessons of earlier revelation were crowned by the 1—4.
coming of Him who was not servant but Son, the
Maker and Heir of the world.   He shews how the Hebr. i.
angels, through whose ministry the Law was 5—14.
given, waited to do homage to Him, proclaimed
King of the renovated order.   He shews how our Hebr. ii.
responsibility as Christians corresponds with the 1—4.
grandeur of the Truth which is placed within our
reach.   He shews how nothing is taken from the Hebr. ii.
universal range of man's dominion, but—and this 5—18.

2—2

II.   is his peculiar message—that it must be reached, that it has been reached, through suffering.

So the writer of the Epistle met at once the central difficulty of the Hebrews. The Hebrews since they believed had been doomed outwardly to the bitterest disappointment. They had looked for a national welcome and they found themselves outcasts; for sovereignty, and they were the victims of popular outrage; for visible triumph, and, as the years went on, they were required to endure *as seeing*, through the thicker gathering gloom, *Him who is invisible.*

Hebr. xi. 27.

And he meets the difficulty by facing it in its fullest form. He passes from the sorrows of Israel to the sorrows of humanity. He quotes from the Psalter a description of the destiny, the position, the hope of man, which answers alike to the noblest aspiration and to the saddest experience. He sets forth the purpose of GOD in creation, and the failure of the creature, and then the triumph of Christ through suffering. In doing this he places in sharpest contrast what was promised to humanity and the actual condition of things. He abates nothing of the inspired estimate of man's nature, and honour, and sovereignty; but at the same time he claims no premature accomplishment of the promise assured to him.   *We see not yet,* he confesses,

Hebr. ii. 8 f.

all things subjected to him. So far there is failure,   II.
failure though the Christ has come. *But we* do
behold . . . Jesus—the Son of man—*because
of the suffering of death crowned with glory and
honour.* There is the spring and the pattern of
attainment, the interpretation of the shame and
of the Passion of the Christ, which is for all time
the interpretation of every grief that clouds the
world, the pledge that the Divine counsel of love
will not fail of fulfilment.

For, as we have already seen, the writer of
the Epistle, when he met the difficulties of the
Hebrews, meets difficulties which press sorely
upon us. Time has not softened the sharpness of
the impression which is made upon thoughtful
spectators by the sight of the sorrows of life. If
the contrast between man made *a little lower than
angels*—nay literally *a little less than GOD*—and Ps. viii. 5
man as man has made him, was startling at the (R. V.).
time when the Apostle wrote, it has not grown
less impressive since.   Larger knowledge
of man's capacities and of his growth, of his
endowments and of his conquests, has only given
intensity to the colours in which poets and
moralists have portrayed the conflict in his nature
and in his life. Whether we look within or
without, we cannot refuse to acknowledge both the
element of nobility in man which bears witness to

II.   his Divine origin, and also the element of selfishness which betrays his fall.   Every philosophy of
humanity which leaves out of account the one or
the other is shattered by experience.   The
loftiest enthusiasm leaves a place in its reconstruc-
tion of society where superstition may attach
itself.   Out of the darkest depths of crime not
seldom flashes a light of self-sacrifice, like the
prayer of the rich man for his brethren when he
was in torments, which shews that all is not
lost.   We cannot accept the theory of
those who see around them nothing but the signs
of unlimited progress towards perfection, or the
theory of those who write a sentence of despair
over the chequered scenes of life.   We look, as
the Psalmist looked, at the sun and the stars, with
a sense which he could not have of the awful
mysteries of the depths of night, but we refuse to
accept space as a measure of being.   We trace
back, till thought fails, the long line of ages
through which the earth was prepared to be our
dwelling-place, but we refuse to accept time as a
measure of the soul.   We recognise without reserve the influence upon us of our ancestry
and our environment, but we refuse to distrust the
immediate consciousness of our personal responsibility.   We do not hide from ourselves any of the
evils which darken the face of the world, but we

Luke xvi.
27 f.

do not dissemble our kindred with the worst and II.
lowest, whose life enters into our lives at a
thousand points.　　　We acknowledge that
the whole creation groaneth and travaileth in pain Rom. viii.
together until now, but we believe also that these 22.
travail pains prepare the joy of a new birth.　We
make no effort to cast off the riddles or the
burdens of our earthly state, but we cling all the
while to the highest thoughts which we have
known as the signs of GOD'S purpose for ourselves
and for our fellow-men.　We allow that man and
men are uncrowned or discrowned in the midst of
their domain, but we hold that they cannot put
off the prerogatives of their birth.　　　We
ask, as prophet and apostle asked : *What,* O Lord,
*is man that Thou art mindful of him? or the son
of man that Thou visitest him?* without any
expectation that we shall find an answer to
the questions ; but none the less we proclaim what
we know, and confess that He is mindful of us,
that He has visited us, that *the Word became* John i. 14.
*flesh and tabernacled among us, full of grace and
truth.*

　And indeed this Gospel reconciles the antago-
nisms of life.　The fact of the Incarnation shews
the possibilities of our nature as GOD made it.
The fact of the Passion shews the issues of sin,
which came from the self-assertion of the creature.

II.

The fact of the Resurrection shews the triumph of love through death.   Christ, in a word, fulfilled man's destiny, fellowship with GOD, by the way of sorrow; and the Divine voice appeals to us to recognise the fitness of the road. *It became Him*—most marvellous phrase—*It became Him for whom are all things, and through whom are all things, in bringing many sons unto glory to make the Author of their salvation perfect through sufferings.*

Hebr. ii. 10; comp. c. vii. 26.

When we ponder these words we shall all come to feel, I think, that they have a message for us on which we have not yet dwelt with the patient thought that it requires, though we greatly need its teaching.   The currents of theological speculation have led us to consider the sufferings of Christ in relation to GOD as a propitiation for sin, rather than in relation to man as a discipline, a consummation of humanity.   The two lines of reflection may be indeed, as I believe they are, more closely connected than we have at present been brought to acknowledge.   I do not however wish now to discuss the propitiatory aspect of the sacrifice of Christ's life.   It is enough for us to remember with devout thankfulness that *Christ is the propitiation not for our sins only, but for the whole world,* without further attempting to define how His sacrifice was

1 John ii. 2.

efficacious. We move on surer ground, when we endeavour to regard that perfect sacrifice from the other side, as the hallowing of every power of man under the circumstances of a sin-stained world, as the revelation of the mystery of sorrow and pain. Of this truth the writer of the Epistle assumes that we are competent judges. He appeals to our natural sense of its 'fitness.' Again and again he presents the thought as the motive and the issue of the Incarnation. He shews that the Advent fulfilled the words of the Psalm: *Lo! I am come to do Thy will, O Lord,* .... *a body didst Thou prepare for me;* and he describes the whole sum of the Lord's earthly work in a phrase which, if we can take it to our hearts, must become a transfiguring of life: *though He was Son, He yet learned obedience by the things which He suffered, and having been made perfect*— perfect by suffering—*He became to all that obey Him the Author of eternal salvation.*

Yes, Christ, *though He was Son,* and therefore endowed with right of access for Himself to the Father, being of one essence with the Father, for man's sake, as man, won the right of access to the throne of GOD for perfected humanity. *He learnt obedience,* not as if the lesson were forced upon Him by stern necessity, but by choosing, through insight into the Father's will, that self-surrender,

II.

c. x. 5 ff.

c. v. 8 f.

II.   even to the death upon the Cross, which was required for the complete reconciliation of man with GOD. And so the absolute union of human nature, in its fullest maturity, with the Divine, in the one Person of our Creator and Redeemer, was wrought out in the very school of life in which we are trained.

When once we grasp this truth the records of the Evangelists are filled with a new light. Every work of Christ is seen to be a sacrifice and a victory. The long years of obscure silence, the short season of conflict, are found to be alike a

John xvii. 19. commentary on the Lord's words, *For their sakes I sanctify myself.* And we come to understand how His deeds of power were deeds of sovereign sympathy; how the words in which Isaiah spoke of the Servant of the Lord, as

Is. liii. 4; Matt. viii. 17. Comp. John i. 29. "taking our infirmities and bearing our sicknesses," were indeed fulfilled when the Son of man healed the sick who came to Him, healed them not by dispensing from His opulence a blessing which cost Him nothing, but by making His own the ill which He removed.

Dimly, feebly, imperfectly, we can see in this way how it *became GOD to make the Author of our salvation perfect through sufferings;* how every pain which answered to the Father's will, became to Him the occasion of a triumph, the disciplining

of some human power which needed to be brought   II.
into GOD's service, the advance one degree farther
towards the Divine likeness to gain which man Gen. i. 26.
was made; how, in the actual condition of the
world, His love and His righteousness were
displayed in tenderer grace and grander authority
through the gainsaying of enemies; how, in this
sense, even within the range of our imagination,
He saw of the travail of His soul and was satisfied. Is. liii. 11.

Dimly, feebly, imperfectly we can see also how
Christ, Himself perfected through suffering, has
made known to us once for all the meaning, and
the value of suffering; how He has interpreted it
as a Divine discipline, the provision of a Father's
love; how He has enabled us to perceive that at
each step in the progress of life it is an oppor-
tunity; how He has left to us to realise "in Him"
little by little the virtue of His work; *to fill up* Col. i. 24.
on our part, in the language of St Paul, *that which
is lacking of the afflictions of Christ* in our own
sufferings, not as if His work were incomplete
or our efforts meritorious, but as being living
members of His Body through which He is
pleased to manifest that which He has wrought
for men.

For we shall observe that it was because He
brought *many sons to glory*, that *it became GOD to
make perfect through sufferings the Author of their*

II.   *salvation.* The fitness lay in the correspondence
between the outward circumstances of His life
and of their lives. The way of the Lord is the way
of His servants. He enlightened the path which
they must tread, and shewed its end.   And
so it is that whenever the example of Christ is
offered to us in Scripture for our imitation, it is
e. g. 1 Pet. His example in suffering. So far, in His strength,
ii. 21.
we can follow Him, learning obedience as He
learned it, bringing our wills into conformity with
the Father's will, and thereby attaining to a
wider view of His counsel in which we can find
rest and joy.

We must dare to face this solemn fact. For
the most part we are tempted to look to the
Gospel for the remission of the punishment of
sins, and not for the remission of sins. But such
a Gospel would be illusory. If the sin remains,
punishment is the one hope of the sinner; if the
sin is forgiven and the light of the Father's love
falls upon the penitent, the punishment, which is
seen as the expression of His righteous wisdom, is
borne with gladness.   Responsive love
transfigures that which it bears. Pain loses its
sting when it is mastered by a stronger passion.
The true secret of happiness is not to escape toil
and affliction, but to meet them with the faith
that through them the destiny of man is fulfilled,

that through them we can even now reflect the image of our Lord and be transformed into His likeness.

II.
2 Cor. iii. 18.

For the power of love is not limited by its personal effects. It goes out upon others with a healing virtue. Not only does the mother know no weariness in ministering to her child, but the sympathy of a friend can change the sorrow which it shares. So love kindles love; and, in the world such as we see it, suffering feeds the purifying flame. Was I not right then when I said that the thought of Christ perfected through suffering, does indeed bring light into the darkest places of the earth? In that light, suffering, if I may so speak, appears as the fuel of love. Up to a certain point we can clearly perceive how the vicissitudes, the sadnesses, the trials of life, become the springs of its tenderness and strength and beauty; how the stress of the campaign calls out the devotion of him whom we had only known as a self-indulgent lounger; how a cry of wrong stirs the spirit of a nation with one resolve; how a cry of agony is answered by the spontaneous confession of human kinsmanship; how the truest joys which we have experienced have come when we have had grace to enter most entirely into a sorrow not our own. And even where sight fails, the virtue of the

II.	Lord's life made perfect through suffering guides us still. We know that not one day of His hidden discipline was fruitless. Each had its lesson of obedience; each marked a fresh advance in the consummation of manhood. So taught, we can feel how the lonely sufferer is still a fellow-worker with Him; how in the stillness of the night-watches a sleepless voice of intercession, unheard by man, but borne to GOD by a "surrendered soul," may bring strength to combatants wearied with a doubtful conflict; how John iv. 37. the word "one soweth and another reapeth," may find a larger application than we have dreamed of, so that when we wake up we may be allowed to see that not one pang in the innumerable woes of men has been fruitless in purifying energy.

Looking then to Christ, Born, Crucified, Risen, Ascended, we can look also on the chequered scene of human life without dissembling one dark trait or abandoning one hope, and claim, in spite of every sign of present disorder, the promise of man's universal dominion as the watchword of our labour. *We see not yet all things subjected to Him; but we behold . . . Jesus because of the suffering of death crowned with glory and honour. . .* And again looking at the conditions of our own life, we can confess through the experience of quickened love that the Gospel justifies itself : that *it became Him, for whom are all things, and through whom are all things, in bringing many sons unto glory, to make the Author of their salvation perfect through sufferings.*

III.

THE KING PRIEST.

Having then a great high priest, who hath passed through the heavens, Jesus the Son of GOD, *let us hold fast our confession.   For we have not a high priest that cannot be touched with the feeling of our infirmities; but one that hath been in all points tempted like as we are, yet without sin.   Let us therefore draw near with boldness unto the throne of grace, that we may receive mercy, and may find grace to help us in time of need.*

HEBR. IV. 14—16.

For such a high priest became us, holy, guileless, undefiled, separated from sinners, and made higher than the heavens.

HEBR. VII. 26.

Now in the things which we are saying the chief point is this: We have such a high priest, who sat down on the right hand of the throne of the Majesty in the heavens.

HEBR. VIII. 1.

THE KING PRIEST.

NO thoughtful person can seriously regard the circumstances of his life without feeling the need of forgiveness and the need of strengthening. He looks back upon the past and he sees not only failures, but unnecessary failures. " He has done what he ought not to have done, and he has not done what he ought to have done." He looks forward to the future, and he sees that while the difficulties of duty do not grow less with added years, the freshness of enthusiasm fades away, and the temptation to accept a lower standard of action grows more powerful. Perhaps in the words of Hood's most touching lyric, he thinks " he's farther off from heaven Than when he was a boy." At any rate, he does feel that in himself he has not reached and cannot reach that for which he was born, that which the spirit of divine discontent within him, a discontent made keener by temporal success, still marks as his one goal of

III. peace. For when Augustine said, *Tu nos fecisti ad te, Domine, et inquietum est cor nostrum donec requiescat in te,*—"Thou, O Lord, hast made us for Thyself, and our heart is restless till it find rest in Thee "—he proclaimed a fact to which every soul bears witness in the silence of its self-communings. We know that we were made for GOD; we know that we have been separated from GOD; we know that we cannot acquiesce in the desolation of that divorce.

We know, I say, that we have been separated from GOD. The sense of this separation makes itself felt in two ways. When we reflect what GOD is and what we are, we shrink from His presence, and we confess that we are unworthy to do Him service. At the same time, by a splendid contradiction, we still seek instinctively for some way of access by which we may draw near to Him, and for some channel of grace through which our sin-stained tribute may be brought before His throne.

So it has been that men in every age have made priests for themselves, to stand between them and their GOD, to offer in some acceptable form the sacrifices which are the acknowledgment of sin, and the gifts which are the symbol of devotion. The institution of the priesthood has been misused, degraded, overlaid with terrible superstitions, but in its essence it corresponds

with the necessities of our nature. Therefore it III.
has been interpreted and fulfilled in the Bible.
And we can yet learn much from the figures of
the Levitical system in which the priesthood *of this* Hebr. ix.
world was fashioned by the Spirit of GOD in a form 1.
of marvellous significance and beauty.   The
law of the priestly service in the Old Testament
is indeed a vivid parable of the needs, the aim,
the benediction of human life. Day by day, Num.
morning and evening, the broad lessons of atone- xxviii. 3 ff.
ment and consecration were read with simple and
solemn emphasis; and once in the year, on the
Great Day of Atonement, " the Day," as it was Lev. xvi.
called, the lessons were set forth in detail with
every accessory of majestic ritual, so that the
simplest worshipper could hardly fail to take to
himself with intelligent faith the warnings and
the consolations of the august ceremonial. On
that day, as will be remembered, the High Priest,
after elaborate cleansings, for himself, for his
family, and for the people, arrayed in white robes,
entered, in the virtue of a surrendered life, into
the dark chamber, which GOD was pleased to
make His dwelling place, and offered incense in
the golden censer, and sprinkled the blood, and
uttered aloud, according to tradition, on that
occasion only, the most sacred Name ; and then,
after completing the purification of the whole

III.

Temple, he dismissed into the wilderness the scape-goat on which he had laid the sins of the people.   On that day, though but for a passing moment, Israel in their representative appeared before the revealed presence of the Lord their GOD.   On that day they received from Him most directly the assurance of forgiveness and blessing—*mercy and grace to help in time of need.*

Hebr. iv. 16.

Now we can, I think, all understand what must have been the consolation, the strength, the joy, with which that service inspired the faithful Jew ; how it must have spoken peace in the name of Jehovah to the troubled conscience, and brought vigour to the trembling ; how, as the passing weeks added weight to the burden of remembered sins, the people must have looked forward to the message brought again from the innermost sanctuary of Truth, that the divine compassion was as vast as their distress ; how in the power of that visible pardon they would, within a few days, join in the Feast of Taber-nacles, " the holiest and greatest " of all their festivals, and shew for a brief space the gladness of social life fulfilled by the gift and in the sight of GOD.

We can understand all this ; and therefore, when we make the effort, we can understand what

the Hebrew Christians must have felt when they
found themselves at last excluded from all share
in this consolation, this strength, this joy, which
they had known from their childhood.

Here was a trial which reached to the very
foundation of their spiritual life. It was not only
that they were condemned to suffering; that
might be a beneficent chastening of sons. But
they seemed to be bereft of the appointed
assurance, given in a form suited to the conditions
of earth, that GOD was accessible to man.

This was a distress which called for a deep-
reaching remedy; and the writer of the Epistle
meets it as he meets all distress. He does not
direct his readers as he might have done, and the
fact calls for careful thought, to the outward
institutions of the Christian society; he does not
shew how provision had been made by the love of
GOD to bring the power of the Gospel to bear on
the whole range of human life, outward and
inward; he does not point out how sacraments as
revelations of the eternal go immeasurably beyond
types which are prophecies of the future. He leads
the Hebrews in their forlorn loneliness at once
to Christ, to *Jesus, the Son of GOD*. He Hebr. iv.
recognises with tender sympathy, he alone we 14.
must notice of the apostolic writers, the grace and
the splendour of the old order; he dwells with

III.

reverent memory on the significance of the ritual which he had known; and then he shews how to the Christian every symbol had become a truth, every shadow a reality, every imaged hope a fact in a perfect human life; he shews how the sacrifice of Christ was efficacious for ever, "one act at once;" how the humanity of Christ was a new and living way to the Father; how on the divine throne placed above the opened heavens, Hebr. vii. 16. was seated One who was Priest *according to the power of an indissoluble life.*

In doing this he carries forward the line of revelation which we have already considered. The work of Christ on earth was the preparation for His work in heaven.

He who fulfilled the destiny of man, under the conditions of the present world; He who interpreted the discipline of suffering; He who bore humanity through death to the presence of GOD— not as one man of men, but as the Head of the Hebr. ii. 17. whole race—did all this *that He might be a merciful and faithful High Priest,* and that He might Hebr. ii. 11. apply to those whom He was *not ashamed to call brethren,* the virtue of His Life and Passion, and reconcile in a final harmony the inexorable claims of law, and the infinite yearnings of love, a Priest and yet a King.

For indeed at first and at last the kingly and

priestly offices cannot be kept apart. The com-   III.
bination which meets us in the simplest forms of
society meets us again when humanity is seen to
have reached its goal. The truth which is thus
expressed lies deep in the facts of life. It answers
to the connexion of the seen and the unseen.
He who makes atonement must direct action.
He who demands the complete service of every
power must hallow the powers of which He claims
the ministry. The ruler who consecrates, the
priest who rules, must, in the words already
quoted, be *merciful and faithful* ; He must have
absolute authority and perfect sympathy; authority that He may represent GOD to man, sympathy
that He may represent man to GOD. And such
is Christ made known to us, King and Priest,
Priest after the order of Melchisedek, in whose   Hebr.v.10;
mysterious person the old world on the edge of a   vi. 20.
new dispensation met and blessed the father of   Hebr. vii.
the faithful.   Therefore the writer of the   1 ff.
Epistle once again is able to appeal to the human
conscience to justify the Gospel. Therefore he
can say, when he has shewn what Christ is, *able*   Hebr. vii.
to save to the uttermost with royal power, *ever*   25 ff.
living to make intercession with priestly compassion; *such a High Priest became us*—we with
our poor faculties can see how He answers to our
wants—*holy* in Himself, *guileless* among men,

III.   *undefiled* in a corrupt world, *separated from sinners* in the conflicts of this visible order, *and made higher than the heavens...a Son perfected for evermore.*

Yes: the apostolic words are true for us, true while there is one sin to vex the overburdened conscience, one struggle to strain the feeble will, *such a High Priest became us.* And it is well for us to turn again and again with reverent devotion to Him as we know, and that we may know better, our faults and our weakness.

We need not dwell long upon His authority. Son of GOD in His own essential nature, He vindicated His Sonship among men. He brought humanity at each stage of His advancing life into perfect fellowship with GOD, offering a perfect service as well as a perfect sacrifice, and then at

John xix. 34.   last—most marvellous paradox—He offered Himself in death upon the cross, and living through death, His earthly work ended, He entered on the

Hebr. viii. 1.   glory of His eternal priesthood, and *sat down on the right hand of GOD.*

cc. i. 3, 13; viii. 1; x. 12; xii. 2.   That single phrase " *sat down on the right hand of GOD,*" on which the writer of the Epistle dwells with solemn emphasis, marks the unique dignity of the ascended Christ. Priests stand in their ministry; angels stand or fall prostrate before the Divine Majesty; but the Son shares the Father's

throne. As Priest, as Intercessor, He reigns still,   III.
reigns in His glorified manhood.

There is our reassurance. Our Priest is King,
and our King is Priest. *The Son of GOD* is also
Jesus, the Son of man. His tender compassion is
infinite even as His authority. We know now
that what Ezekiel saw in a vision has become for Ezek. i. 26.
us a fact. We see by faith upon the sapphire
throne not the shadowy likeness of a man, but
One who is true man; One who was *made in all* Hebr. ii.
things like unto His brethren; One who was 17.
tempted in all things after our likeness; One who Hebr. iv.
has known the bitterness of every human trial, 15.
and who knows the secret of their use; One
whose sympathy goes out to every suffering
creature as if he were alone the object of His
regard; One whose love kindles to responsive
warmth the faintest spark of faith.

We can feel then how the Hebrews through
their apparent loss were brought to an immeasurable gain, and how we may learn a little better
through their example what our King-Priest is for
us.

If human priests compassed with infirmity
could inspire confidence in the worshipper, then
Christ, if we will lift our eyes to Him, a thousand-
fold more. Their compassion was necessarily Hebr. v.
limited by their experience, but His experience 1 ff.

III.   covers the whole field of life ; their gentle bearing
was tempered by the consciousness of personal
failure, but His breathes the invigorating spirit of
perfect holiness. They knew the power of temptation in part by the sad lessons of failure ; He knew
it to the uttermost by perfect victory. They
could see dimly through earth-born mists something of the real hideousness of evil ; He
saw it in the undimmed light of the Divine
purity.   And He is tenderest, not who
has sinned, as is sometimes vainly thought, but
who has known best the power of sin by over-
coming it. His love is most watchful who has
seen what wrong is in the eyes of GOD.

Can we not then boldly proclaim that here
also the Gospel covers the facts of life, of our life ?
that in the prospect of the conflicts and defeats
which sadden us, and which we dare not disguise
or extenuate, *such a High Priest became us*, strong
with the strength of GOD, compassionate with the
affection of a friend ?

Gen.xxxii. 24 ff.   We must cling to both these truths, and
wrestle with them, and win their blessing from
them. We need the revelation of Christ's Majesty
and we need the revelation of Christ's Tenderness.
We need more, I think, than we know, to come
each one of us into the presence of the glorified
Lord and rest in His light.

In this individual approach to the throne of ⅲ. grace lies for us severally the promise of the fulfilment of our destiny. But "earth's children cling to earth," and there are many among us who feel keenly the very trials which the Hebrews felt; who long for some visible system which shall "bring all heaven before their eyes," for some path to the divine presence along which they can walk by sight, for recurrent words of personal absolution from some human minister, for that which shall localise their centre of worship; who labour, often unconsciously, to make the earthly the measure of the spiritual; who shrink from the ennobling responsibility of striving with untiring effort to hold communion with the unseen and eternal; who turn back with regretful looks to the discipline and the helps of a childly age, when they are required to accept the graver duties of maturity; required to listen, as it were, like Elijah on the lonely mountain, when the 1 K. xix. thunder of the earthquake is stilled and the ¹² violence of the fire is spent, for the still small voice.

These are not, I know, imaginary temptations; but if we are tried and disquieted by their assaults, the writer of the Epistle enables us to face them. He brings Christ near to us and he brings us near to Christ. He discloses the privileges to which

III.

John xiv.
9.

Hebr. iv.
14 ff.

we are all admitted by the ascended Saviour.
He gives an abiding application to the Lord's
words, *He that hath seen Me hath seen the
Father.*   And he does this without hiding
one dark trait in the prospect of life. The connexion in which the text stands gives it a startling
force. The apostolic author has recalled without
reserve, the sad history of Israel's failure. He
has painted a vivid picture of the penetrating
severity of the Divine judgment, and then, draw-
ing an unexpected conclusion from this revelation
of unbelief and weakness and retribution, he continues: *Having therefore a great High Priest who
hath passed through the heavens, Jesus the Son of
GOD, let us hold fast our confession. For we have
not a High Priest that cannot be touched with the
feeling of our infirmities; but one that hath been in
all points tempted like as we are, yet without sin.
Let us therefore draw near with boldness unto the
throne of grace, that we may receive mercy and
may find grace to help in time of need.*

Every word must go to the heart of those who
have known what life is, an inexorable order
capable of being transfigured by love. Every
word has a practical force. Never was the charge
to hold fast our confession more urgently needed.
Never was the encouragement to come directly to
Christ more fitted to still the griefs of failure, and

to nerve the misgivings of weakness.   Never was
the twofold necessity of rising out of themselves
without losing themselves more impressively forced
upon men by the contrast between their ideal and
their attainment, their destiny and their position;
never was the Spirit more openly claiming acceptance for growing Truth.

As then we have known a little of the power
of our Faith; as we have felt the want of forgiveness and the want of support; as we have learnt
a little more clearly with advancing years the
grievousness of sin and the perils of life, *let us,*
each in our place, *hold fast our confession.*

*Let us draw near with boldness to the throne of
grace*—giving utterance to every feeling and every
wish—*that we may receive mercy*—receive it as
humble suppliants from the Lord's free love—*and
may find*—find as unwearied searchers—*grace to
help in time of need.*

That access is ever open to the foot of faith.
That mercy is unfailing to the cry of penitence.
That grace is inexhaustible to the servant who
offers himself wholly to the Master's use.

IV.

THE UNIVERSAL SOCIETY.

Ye are come unto mount Zion, and unto the city of the living GOD, the heavenly Jerusalem, and to innumerable hosts of angels, to the general assembly and church of the firstborn who are enrolled in heaven, and to GOD the Judge of all, and to the spirits of just men made perfect, and to Jesus the mediator of a new covenant, and to the blood of sprinkling that speaketh better than that of Abel.

HEBR. XII. 22—24.

THE UNIVERSAL SOCIETY.

WE have seen that the solemn and consolatory lessons of the priestly service of the Old Testament, which were brought together in their highest form on the Day of Atonement, obtained their fulfilment in the work of Christ. We have seen that Christ realised in the victorious progress of a perfect life that absolute holiness, of which ceremonial cleansings were a figure; that He, uniting in one Person the offices of priest and victim, *through the eternal Spirit, offered* the humanity which He had taken to Himself, a sacrifice well-pleasing to GOD upon the altar of the Cross, *not for the nation only,* but for the world; that through the grave, and through the heavens, He bore His own blood, the virtue of His Manhood given for men, to the immediate presence of GOD, pleading on our behalf for ever; that going infinitely beyond the privilege of intercession by that one entrance, He sat down

Hebr. ix. 14; xiii. 10.

John xi. 52. Hebr. iv. 14.

4—2

v.   as Divine King on the Father's throne, crowning the ministry of priestly compassion with the glory of universal sovereignty.

So far the types of the Day of Atonement have been fulfilled, and far more than fulfilled; but the last scene in the august ceremonial of the day has not at present found its counterpart. Our High Priest has not yet returned from the heavenly sanctuary to reveal on earth the completeness of His work in visible triumph.   Our position therefore is, in one sense, like that of the congregation of Israel gathered round the Holy Place, waiting with eager and beating hearts till their representative should come forth to bring again before their sight the fact of forgiveness and acceptance.   We too are in an attitude of

Hebr. ii. 8.   expectancy.   *We see not yet all things subjected* to our Redeemer.   Clouds and darkness are over the world which is His inheritance; and we look for Him, in the words of the Epistle, when He

Hebr. ix. 28.   *shall appear a second time apart from sin, to them that wait for Him, unto salvation.*

This, I say, is one aspect of our position.   We are in an attitude of expectancy; and in this respect it is of the utmost importance that we should keep our brightest hopes fresh, and neither dissemble the sorrows of life, nor surrender the

2 Cor. iv. 7.   least of the Divine promises.   *We walk by faith,*

not by sight. But the reality, the inten- IV.
sity, of our expectancy must not hide from us the
reality of our attainment. If the appearance of
Christ is future, fellowship with Him and with
His people is present. *Ye are come,* the author Hebr. xii.
of the Epistle writes to men troubled by doubts, 22.
by divisions, by losses, by sufferings, as grievous
as any which we have to bear, by shamelessness
of triumphant vice to which Christendom offers
no parallel, *Ye are come*—and not, "Ye shall come"
—*unto mount Zion, and unto the city of the living
GOD, the heavenly Jerusalem, . . . and to Jesus the
Mediator of a new covenant. . . .* He writes, I
repeat, "Ye are come," and not, "Ye shall come,"
and no blindness, no faithlessness, can alter the
fact.

The Hebrews were, as we remember, in danger
of forgetting the grandeur of their privilege
under the stress of temporal affliction, and so the
Apostle recalls the most memorable scene in their
sacred history. He contrasts the beginnings of
Judaism, and the beginnings of Christianity; the
character of the old kingdom of GOD imaged in the
circumstances of its foundation, and the character
of the new kingdom made clear in its spiritual
glory through tribulations and chastenings, that
they might see what the Gospel was not as well
as what it was. *Ye are not come,* he says, *unto*

IV.   *a palpable and kindled fire, and unto blackness,
and darkness, and tempest, and the sound of a
trumpet, and the voice of words.* ... Ye are not
come, that is, like your forefathers, to an outward,
earthly, elemental manifestation of the Divine
Majesty, which appealed to the senses, and even
where it was most intelligible and most human,
struck those to whom it was given with overwhelming dread; *but ye are come unto mount Zion,
and unto the city of the living* GOD, *the heavenly
Jerusalem, and to innumerable hosts of angels, to
the general assembly and church of the firstborn
who are enrolled in heaven.* ... Ye are come, come
already, come even if GOD seems to hide Himself,
to a Divine Presence nearer and more pervading
than Moses knew; to an abiding communion
realised in vital energy, and not to a passing vision
shewn in material forces; to a revelation marked,
as the Apostle goes on to shew, not by threatening
commands, but by means of reconciliation, inspiring
not fear but love.

Now when we reflect upon the contrast, we
shall be led to perceive that it could not fail to
suggest thoughts of reassurance to the Hebrews.
They were, it is true, shut out, irrevocably shut
out, from the courts of the Temple, deprived of
the friendship of those who claimed to be the
children of the patriarchs and the prophets,

outcasts from the visible commonwealth of GOD. IV.
But what then? When they lost these
earthly privileges, which gave a transient satisfaction to their souls, they were taught even through
their grief to gain a larger vision of the Divine
action and of the Divine presence; to see through
the typical splendours of the vanishing sanctuary,
the city that hath the foundations, of which every Hebr. xi.
institution of earth is a partial shadow; to see 10.
Hebr. xii.
about them the great cloud of witnesses who 1 f.
proclaim that not one aspiration of faith has ever
failed of attainment; to see on the right hand of
the Father—that right hand which is everywhere—Him in whom all creation finds its unity
and its life, Jesus, Son of man and Son of GOD,
accessible to each believer; to see that Christianity
is not an etherialised Judaism, but its spiritual
antitype; that the heavenly Jerusalem is no
material locality, but the realm of eternal truth;
that the Christian society is not in essence an
external organisation, but a manifestation of the
powers of the new life.

And for us this teaching has, I think, a still
wider application. The spectacle of divided and
rival Churches is as sad and far vaster than the
spectacle of unbelieving Israel. It is hard
for us to bear the prospect of Christendom rent
into hostile fragments as it was hard for the

IV.

Hebrews to bear the anathema of their country-men. It is hard to look for peace, and to find a sword; to look for the concentration of every force of those who bear Christ's name in a common assault upon evil, and to find energies of thought and feeling and action weakened and wasted in misunderstandings, jealousies, and schisms; to look for the beauty of a visible unity of the faithful which shall strike even those who are without with reverent awe, and to find our divisions a commonplace with mocking adver-saries.   It is hard; and, if what we see were all, the trial would be intolerable. But what we see is not all: what we see is not even the dim image of that which is. The life which we feel, the life which we share, is more than the earthly materials by which it is at present sustained, more than the earthly vestures through which it is at present manifested. That is not most real which can be touched and measured, but that which struggles, as it were, to find imperfect expression through the veil of sense; that which to the All-seeing Eye gilds with the light of self-devotion acts that to us appear self-willed and miscalculated; that which to the All-hearing Ear joins in a full harmony words that to us sound fretful and impatient; that which fills our poor dull hearts with a love and sympathy

John xvii. 21.

towards all the creatures of GOD, deeper than   IV
just hatred of sin, deeper than right condemnation
of error, deeper than the circumstances of birth
and place and temperament, which kindle the
friendships and sharpen the animosities of human
intercourse.

Yes : the unseen and the eternal is for all of us
who confess Christ come, Christ coming in flesh, 1 John iv.
the ruling thought of life. To us also the words 7.
are spoken—*Ye are come unto mount Zion, and
unto the city of the living GOD, the heavenly Jerusalem, and to innumerable hosts of angels, to the
general assembly and church of the firstborn who
are enrolled in heaven ; and to the GOD of all as
Judge, and to the spirits of just men made perfect,
and to Jesus the Mediator of a new covenant, and to
the blood of sprinkling which speaketh better than
that of Abel.*

Ye are come, that is, come though your way
seems to be barred by inevitable obstacles, though
your prospect seems to be closed by impenetrable
gloom, to a scene of worship and a company of
fellow-worshippers which no eye hath seen nor
can see ; ye are come to powers of the spiritual
order which are able to bring assurance in the
midst of the confusions, the uncertainties, the
failures, by which you are wearied and perplexed ;
ye are come, in a word, to a dispensation, not

iv.   earthly but heavenly, to a dispensation not of
terror but of grace.

Each of these two characteristics of the Divine
order to which we are admitted, that it is heavenly,
and that it is gracious, has for us, as for the
Hebrews, a message of encouragement.

If the outward were the measure of the Church
of Christ, we might, as we have seen, well despair.
But side by side with us, when we fondly think,
1 K. xix. 14, 18. like Elijah, or Elisha's servant, that we stand
2 K. vi. 17. alone, are countless multitudes whom we know
not, angels whom we have no power to discern,
children of GOD whom we have not learnt to
recognise.   We are come to the kingdom of GOD,
peopled with armies of angels and men working
for us and with us because they are working
for Him.   And though we cannot grasp
the fulness of the truth, and free ourselves from
the fetters of sense, yet we can, in the light of the
Incarnation, feel the fact of this unseen fellowship ;
we can feel that heaven has been re-opened to us
by Christ ; that the hosts who were separated
from Israel at Sinai by the fire and the darkness
are now joined with us under our Saviour King,
John i. 51. *ascending and descending upon the Son of man ;*
that no external tests are final in spiritual things ;
that while we are separated one from another by
barriers which we dare not overpass, by differences

of opinion which we dare not conceal or extenuate, there still may be a deeper-lying bond in *righteousness, peace, and joy in the Holy Ghost,* the apostolic notes of the kingdom of GOD, which nothing that is of earth can for ever overpower.

IV.
Rom. xiv. 17.

Such convictions are sufficient to bring a calm to the believer in the sad conflicts of a restless age, widely different from the blind complacency which is able to forget the larger sorrows of the world in the confidence of selfish security, and from the superficial indifference which regards diversities as trivial, which for good or evil modify the temporal workings of faith.   They enable us to preserve a true balance between the elements of our life.   They teach us to maintain the grave, if limited, issues of the forms in which men receive the truth, and to vindicate for the Spirit perfect freedom and absolute sovereignty.   They guard us from that deceitful impatience which is eager to anticipate the last results of the discipline of the world and gain outward unity by compromise; which is hasty to abandon treasures of our inheritance because we have forgotten or misunderstood their use.   They inspire us with the ennobling hope that in the wisdom of GOD we shall become one, not by narrowing and defining the Faith which is committed to us, but by rising, through the help of the

iv.   Spirit, to a worthier sense of its immeasurable
grandeur.

And yet more than this: they quicken our
common life with a vital apprehension of the
powers of the unseen order; they break the
tyranny of a one-sided materialism; they proclaim
that a belief in natural law is essentially a belief in
a present GOD; they take possession of a region of
being which answers to the capacities of the soul;
they encourage us to bring our ordinary thoughts
and feelings into the light of our eternal destiny,
and add to them that idea of incalculable issues
which must belong to all that is human.

At the same time there is an element of awe in
this revelation of the fulness of spiritual force
active about us, of this association with invisible
fellow-workers, of this communion with Him who
is a consuming fire. And the writer of the Epistle
does not shrink from dwelling on the sterner
aspect of his teaching. He insists on the heavier
responsibility which attaches to those who have
larger knowledge. He calls for the exertion, the
courage, the thoughtful endurance, the watchful
purity, which correspond with the truths that he
has laid open.

Life indeed is filled with awe. Its solemnity
grows upon us. We may wish to remain children
always, but we cannot. And here the Gospel

Hebr. xii.
29.

meets the fears which spring out of the larger
vision of our state. It is heavenly, and it is
gracious too. We have come not only to
an order glorious with spiritual realities, but also
to an order rich in provisions of mercy : *to the*
GOD of all as Judge, and to the spirits of just men
made perfect, and to Jesus the Mediator of a new
covenant, and to the blood of sprinkling which
speaketh better than that of Abel. The words
teach us to look backward and to look forward, and
to draw from the past and from the present the
inspiration of faith. We look to those
whose work is over, we see that judgment is a
deliverance for 'surrendered souls', and that the
work of Christ has brought perfection to His
servants through the sufferings of earth. We
look to those who are still pressed in the fight, and
we see with them Jesus the Son of man, shewing
in His own Person that GOD is their support, and
applying to each the virtue of His own life.

Once again then we are brought to Him, when
our thoughts are turned to the widest mysteries
of life. When we behold the depths of heaven
opened about us, and the veil lifted from the
living fulness of earth, He stands before our face—
stands as He appeared to His first martyr—to
welcome those who follow Him in hope within the
sanctuary of the Divine Presence.

IV.

Hebr. xii.
23 f.

Acts vii.
56.

IV.

Once again He is revealed to us as bringing the help which we need in view of the questions which are forced upon us by the circumstances in which we are placed. We have seen already that He has transfigured suffering, by shewing that it is through suffering humanity is perfected. We have seen that He has consecrated a new and living way for us to GOD, by bearing our manhood to the throne of heaven. We see now that, when we regard the innumerable forms of being which crowd the spiritual temple, He is with us still, to assure us that there is a place for us in that august company and to prepare us for taking it.

Hebr. x. 20.

Once again He is revealed to us as communicating to His people of His own glory for the accomplishment of their destiny. He is the Firstborn, and He gathers round Him *a Church of the firstborn,* in which Divine family each member shares the highest privilege. " Cum pluribus," wrote an early commentator from the solitude of his French convent, "major erit beatitudo; ubi unusquisque de alio gaudebit sicut de seipso." Yes ; " The bliss will be greater when more share it. In heaven each one will rejoice for his fellow as for himself."

Once again He is revealed to us as the Fulfiller —*Christus Consummator*—gathering into one and reconciling all things by the will of GOD.

And let no one think that such a revelation is fitted only to fill the fancy with splendid dreams. It is, I believe, intensely practical. He who leaves the unseen out of account deals as it were with a soulless world, with a mechanical structure of matter and force. But for the Christian all is law, and life, and love. He has *come unto mount Zion, and unto the city of the living GOD, the heavenly Jerusalem, and to innumerable hosts of angels, to the general assembly and church of the firstborn who are enrolled in heaven . . . and to Jesus the Mediator of a new covenant. . . .*

For him the wilderness, desolate to the bodily eye, is thronged with joyous ministers of GOD's will. For him no differences of earth can destroy the sense of kindred which springs from a common spiritual destiny.

What then, we are constrained to ask, is this revelation, what are these facts to us ? Do they not meet the loneliness which has depressed us, the weakness which has often marred our efforts ?

It must be so if GOD, in His love, open our eyes to behold the armies of light by which we are encircled ; if He open our hearts to feel the strength of fellowship with every citizen of His kingdom.

V.

THE NEW COVENANT.

But now hath he obtained a ministry the more excellent, by how much also he is the mediator of a better covenant, which hath been enacted upon better promises.

HEBR. VIII. 6.

We have an altar, whereof they have no right to eat which serve the tabernacle.

HEBR. XIII. 10.

THE NEW COVENANT.

v.

THE attitude of a Christian is, as we have seen,
twofold. It is an attitude of attainment, and
an attitude of expectancy. He has been admitted
to fellowship with the unseen order in the fulness
of its infinite grandeur; and he is looking for the
open manifestation of the victorious Presence of
his Lord.   This inspiring faith, this far-
reaching hope, are bound together for each one of
us by the obligation of personal duty. Each one
of us has a work to do in that infinite kingdom of
GOD which is opened to our entrance. Each one
of us is charged in his measure to hasten the full
revelation of its glory. We look through the
temporal to the eternal.   But for the
present we have to live our little lives under the
conditions of earth. We strive to gain the largest
vision of the Divine counsels, to feel the intense
reality of our connexion with the world about us,
to watch in thought the stream of consequence

2 Pet. iii. 12.

5—2

v. which flows from our actions; and then strengthened and humbled we go back as it were into the shrine of our own souls, and know that in that last depth of being we are alone with GOD. We are alone, and yet not alone; for there also Christ is with us, Christ the Fulfiller, to bring to its true perfection the fragment of service which answers to our powers. He not

Hebr. ix. 12; xii. 24.

only bore His blood, the virtue of His offered life, into heaven for the salvation of the nature which He had taken to Himself, but He applies it personally to each believer on earth, to purify and to sustain, to begin and to complete that union with Himself for which man was made.

As the Hebrews grasped this truth which the Apostle set before them, they could not fail to find that what they had lost by their exclusion from the commonwealth of Israel was given back to them in fact, and not in figure. As Israelites they had rejoiced from early youth to enter the court of GOD's house; as Israelites, they had known in maturer age every consolation of the appointed sacrifices. But now, when they entered little by little into the meaning of the Gospel, they saw that they were become partakers

Hebr. viii. 6.
Hebr. iii. 14; vi. 4.

in a better covenant than that made with their fathers; in a better sacrifice than those which the Law established; "partakers in Christ," "partakers

in the Holy Ghost." They were indeed, what
Israel was designed to be, a nation of priests.
The offering for the people's sin was for them
given back as the support of life.

v.

Hebr. xiii.
10.

The lessons which were thus taught, taught
most impressively through the symbols of the Old
Testament to men tried by the sorrows of the
first age, are for us also.   The individual
soul as it turns to GOD requires to be assured of
the personal right of approach to Him, and then
of the power of continuous fellowship with Him.
This assurance is given to us, in a form suited to
the circumstances of our life, in the two Sacraments of the Gospel—the Sacrament of Incor-
poration, and the Sacrament of Support.   In these
we have, according to our need, the revelation of
our union with Christ and the revelation of His
impartment of Himself to us.

But we cannot fail to be struck by the way in
which the writer of the Epistle deals with these
Sacraments.   We should have expected that he
would contrast them in their significant forms
with the typical Levitical rites to which they
answered; that he would shew how even outwardly the Christian has in them far more sure
seals of GOD's grace than the Jew; that he would
point out that what was necessarily limited and
local in the old dispensation had been made

v.   universal in the new.   As it is, he barely touches
on the external element of the Christian Sacraments.   The external element lies behind
his teaching; but he strives above all things to
fix the thoughts of his readers upon the ascended
Christ who works through the Sacraments, lest
they should rest in ritual observances, and faint
or fail in the effort to gain a closer personal fellowship with Him.

There are, however, two remarkable passages
which enable the student to perceive, as I have
already indicated, the deep meaning of the
Mystical Washing, and of the festal meal of the
Eucharist.   *Let us draw near*—near to the Holy
place—the Apostle writes, *with a true heart in
fulness of faith, having our hearts sprinkled from
an evil conscience, and our body washed with pure
water.*   And again, *We have an altar, whereof
they have no right to eat which serve the tabernacle.*

Hebr. x. 22.

Hebr. xiii. 10.

The first passage shews that by our covenant
rite we are made not only a people of GOD, but
also priests of GOD.

The second passage shews that while the sin-
offering on the Day of Atonement was wholly
consumed by fire, our common sin-offering is made
our common peace-offering, our Eucharist, a Feast
upon a Sacrifice.

Twice only in the Pentateuch is mention made of the sprinkling of the blood of sacrifices upon men; once at the solemn ratification of the covenant, when the people were united to the Lord; and once when Aaron and his sons were hallowed for the priesthood. In the latter case the sprinkling with blood was united with a washing with water. Here then we have the complete parallel with the words of the Epistle. To a Jew, familiar with the Mosaic record, their meaning was distinct and decisive. They set forth that the Christian is made, as I said, not only a citizen of the Divine kingdom, but also a priest of GOD; that for him access to heaven is open; that he has boldness to offer the sacrifices of word and deed; that he accepts the duty of consecration.

The interpretation of the second passage which I have quoted has been disputed, but I think that the general sense is clear. The writer is meeting a difficulty found in the supposition that Christians had not what the Jews had. *We have,* he replies, *an altar,* an altar with a victim, for the two are not separated, *whereof they have no right to eat who serve the tabernacle.* We have, that is, more, infinitely more, than the Law allowed to those who ministered to figures of the eternal truth. We have Christ crucified, Christ upon the Cross,

v.

Ex. xxiv. 8.

Lev. viii. 23 f; 30; 6.

Hebr. xiii. 15 f.

v.   a victim and an altar, a victim who suffered for the world without the camp, and who then, marvel of marvels, gave and gives Himself for ever as the support of His people in a Holy Eucharist.   No priest in old time ever tasted such an offering.   But He who died for us lives for us.   He who bore our sins gives us of the fulness of His strength.   And, to go one step further, on Him and in Him we can bring to GOD the sacrifice of ourselves.

So then, we repeat, our covenant rite, our Baptism, brings us into a personal relation to Christ.   No one stands between the believer and the Lord.   Our Sacrificial Feast, our Eucharist, offers to us the virtue of Christ's life and death, His Flesh and Blood, for the strength-ening and cleansing of our bodies and souls.

Let us look at these thoughts a little more closely.

As baptized, confirmed Christians, priests of GOD, we can come directly to the Father.   No earthly symbol, no mortal representative, inter-venes any longer as the necessary means through which we may draw near.

As baptized, confirmed Christians, priests of GOD, we can offer up to Him a sacrifice of praise and active love, the natural fruit of hearts touched John xv.7. with His grace.   No fear checks the thanksgiving

which is the echo of His word. No weakness   v.
stays the effort which is the answer to His
summons.

As baptized, confirmed Christians, priests of
GOD, we acknowledge that we are *holy, partakers* Hebr. iii.
of a heavenly calling, dedicated to GOD without ¹·
reserve, *bearing branded* upon us, in St Paul's Gal. vi. 17.
vivid image, *the marks of Jesus,* as bondmen
devoted to His perpetual service.

But while this is so; while nothing can alter
the responsibility which is laid upon each soul,
and which we have voluntarily acknowledged;
while we must severally, as if there were none
other, draw near to GOD and bring Him the offering of ourselves, and acknowledge the debt which
is as large as life ; our approach, our sacrifice, our
dedication, are all *in Christ.* Not one step, not
one act, not one confession, can be made without
Him. ` *We are become partakers of Christ.* Hebr. iii.
That is the gift of GOD. And while the Epistle ¹⁴·
recognises, as we have seen, the priesthood of
Christians, this human priesthood falls almost out
of sight before the supreme fact of the priesthood
of Christ. Our common priestly work is done
only through Him. *Through Him we offer up a* Hebr. xiii.
sacrifice of praise to GOD continually. Our will ¹⁵·
makes it our own. His co-operation makes it
acceptable.

v.
Hebr. iii.
14.
We are become partakers of Christ, if, it is
added, *we hold fast the beginning of our confidence
firm unto the end.* A Divine fact, such is the
paradox of life, is made dependent on human
endeavour.   We can see therefore how the
institution of the Eucharist meets the sad sense
of infirmity and failure. Our covenant rite cannot
from its nature ever be repeated. But we know
how often and how grievously we have fallen
short of our obligation. Is the covenant then,
we are driven to ask, fatally broken ?   When the
fear rises before us, we recall, almost regretfully,
the provisions which men have made, with or
without the sanction of GOD, to bring, through
sacrifice, peace to the troubled conscience. While
we do so, the Apostle lifts up our thoughts to
the Lord, Crucified, Risen, Seated at the right
hand of the Father, and in the light of that
Hebr. xiii.
8. vision of *Jesus Christ, the same yesterday and
to-day, yea, and for ever,* we can say triumphantly,
We have an altar.   All that the consolatory
ceremonial of the Old Dispensation accomplished
for Israel, all that men have sought to make clear
to themselves by vain speculations and worldly
forms, is ours in spiritual and abiding simplicity.
We have an altar wherein the truths which were
represented by the sacrificial system of the Law
are realised in a living verity.   *We have an altar,*

whereon we can lay " ourselves, our souls and   v.
bodies," a reasonable service.

Once again then we are brought to Christ the
Fulfiller—*Christus Consummator*—in whom each
believer finds the root and the accomplishment
of his individual destiny.

So, we have reached the limit which we set to
ourselves. We have dared to look upon great
trials in the light of the Epistle to the Hebrews,
and we have seen that the help which availed the
Hebrews in the first age is sufficient for us.

We have looked upon suffering; and we have
seen that by the will of GOD suffering is for fallen
man the way to perfection. We cannot indeed,
with our feeble sight, discern how this or that
sorrow and shame contributes to the end; but
disciplined in patience, we can leave in the Father's
hands the fulfilment of His own law which we
have recognised, and for our part labour to hasten
that issue.

We have looked upon failure and weakness;
and we have seen that Christ, as He accomplished
the destiny of man on earth, pleads the cause of
man in heaven with unfailing compassion and
absolute sovereignty, uniting the offices of priest
and king, perfect man and perfect GOD.

We have looked upon the sad spectacle of

v.   divided Christendom; and we have seen that by
the Ascension of Christ we are brought into a
spiritual fellowship, in which the powers of heaven
and earth are united, a fellowship transcending
every test of sense; and from the contemplation
of the notes of that universal communion, we have
learnt to keep hope fresh while we guard with
watchful reverence the convictions which separate
us in the sphere of visible work.

We have looked upon the chequered course of
the individual life; and we have seen that for each
one of us is provided that objective assurance
of our right of approach to GOD which is the solid
foundation of religion, that objective assurance of
the renewed gift of Christ's flesh and blood, which
is able to sustain and to purify us in the effort to
reach His likeness.

At every prospect of great trial, as we dwelt
patiently upon it, we have seen the figure of
Christ to rise above the darkness—of Christ the
Fulfiller—not only to give comfort, but to enlarge
hope; not only to support the sufferer under the
pressure of transitory affliction, but to shew to the
believing soul that, in a world such as this,

> "Failure is but a triumph's evidence
> For the fulness of the days."

And we have seen all this, so far as we have
been allowed to see it, by entering a little more

closely than is commonly done into the difficulties
of a troubled congregation of the apostolic
times. Thus we have found that the
words of the inspired writer who guided the
Hebrews to higher things, speak to us with the
directness and the power of life. We
have found on a narrow field of inquiry what the
Bible is: an interpretation of the eternal, intelligible to every man through all time in the
language in which he was born. We
have found that nothing has befallen us which our
fathers have not borne victoriously in other shapes,
and made fruitful in blessing. We have
found, I think, that to those who will raise their
eyes to Christ the Fulfiller, the Revelation of the
Father, made known to us more completely from
generation to generation by the Holy Spirit,
nothing in human experience can come as an
unwelcome surprise. He, Son of man, Son of
GOD, will bear, He has borne, though we see it not
through the mist of days and years, all things to
their goal, *Christus Consummator.*

Such thoughts carry with them a grave, a
noble responsibility. The character of a generation is moulded by personal character. And if we
have considered some of the temptations of the
first Christians; if we know a little of the terrible
environment of evil by which they were encircled;

v.

Acts ii. 5 ff.

John xiv.
9.
John xiv.
26.

v.   we must not, as we too often do, forget how they
      conquered the world.   It was not by any
      despairing withdrawal from city and market; not
      by any proud isolation in selfish security; not by
      any impatient violence; but by the winning
      influence of gracious faith, they mastered the
      family, the school, the empire. They were a liv-
      ing Gospel, a message of GOD's good-will to those
      with whom they toiled and suffered.   Pure
      among the self-indulgent, loving among the
      factious, tender among the ruthless, meek among
      the vainglorious, firm in faith amidst the shaking
      of nations, joyous in hope amidst the sorrows of
      a corrupt society, they revealed to men their true
      destiny and shewed that it could be attained.
      They appealed boldly to the awakened conscience
      as the advocate of their claims. They taught as
      believing that He who had stirred their heart
      with a great desire would assuredly satisfy it.

          They offered not in word but in deed, the ideal
      of spiritual devotion, and "the soul naturally
      Christian," turned to it, as the flower turns to the
      light, drew from it, as the flower draws from the
      light, the richness of perfect beauty.

          Yes; that was the secret of their success; and
      it is the secret of our success. The words are true
      now, as they were when addressed by Zechariah to
      the poor remnant of Jews struggling to rebuild

their outward temple: *Not by might, nor by power,* v.
but by My Spirit, saith the Lord of hosts. Not Zech. iv. 6.
first by material change, not by intellectual culture,
but by spiritual sympathy will our work be done.
Let us take to ourselves the charge of our Epistle,
the counsel of Divine fellowship—fellowship with
GOD in man, fellowship with man in GOD. *Let* Hebr. iv.
us draw near unto the throne of grace. . . . Let us 16.
hold fast the confession of our hope. . . . Let us Hebr. x.
consider one another to provoke unto love and good 24.
works, and it shall not be long said that the
victories of faith are ended.

CHRISTUS CONSUMMATOR. II.

ASPECTS OF THE INCARNATION.

But Mary kept all these sayings, pondering them in her heart.

ST LUKE ii. 19.

THE INCARNATION A SUBJECT FOR
DEVOUT STUDY.

THERE is no grander passage in Greek litera- I.
ture than that in which Plato describes how
the contemplation of absolute justice, temperance,
and knowledge is the sustenance of the divine
nature. There are times of high festival, he says,
in the world above, when the gods in solemn *Phædr.*
procession mount to the topmost vault of heaven, p. 246 D.
and, taking their place upon its dome, gaze over
the infinite depths of perfect Truth. This
spectacle supports the fulness of their being.
Nor are they, he continues, alone in the enjoy-
ment of the magnificent vision : all the souls
that can and will follow in their train. Such of
these as are able to gain the fair prospect and
keep it before their eyes, while the spheres revolve,
remain in the possession of supreme joy. The
rest baffled, wearied, maimed, sink down to earth
and are embodied as men. Henceforward,
he adds, their condition in this lower life depends

I.   upon their past apprehension of the Truth. Their
human existence is a striving upwards toward the
glory which they have once seen. They live still,
so far as they really live, by the recollection of
that which has filled them with a noble passion.

The life of man is thus according to the highest thought of Greek philosophy remembered
Truth. Such an intuition of noble souls found
its confirmation and fulfilment in the Presence
John xvii. and in the word of the Lord: *This is,* He
3.   says, *the life eternal—This* is the life, and not
This is its condition, or its foundation, or its
portal, or its preparation—*This is the life eternal,
that they may know*—know, such is the force of
the word, with a knowledge widening from hour to
hour under the discipline of experience and oppor-
tunity—*Thee the only true* GOD, *and Him whom
Thou didst send, even Jesus Christ.*

Yes: the life of man is the knowledge of GOD,
the contemplation of Him Who is the Truth.
That is the message of Christ. But this knowledge lives and moves. It is not a dead thing
embalmed once for all in phrases of the school
which can be committed to memory. It is offered
ever fresh as time advances for reverent study in
the Person of the Word Incarnate.   The
surest knowledge once gained cannot supersede
the necessity of unwearied, unceasing, inquiry.

No one can absolve himself from the duty of spiritual thought.   I.

The words which I have chosen for a text present the duty to us with almost startling force. The Mother of the Lord had received that direct, personal, living, revelation of the purpose and the working of GOD which none other could have : she had acknowledged in the familiar strain of the *Magnificat* the salvation which He had prepared through her for His people : she might well seem to have been lifted far above the necessity of any later teaching ; but when the simple shepherds told their story, a faint echo as we might think of what she knew, she *kept all these things pondering them in her heart,* if haply they might shew a little more of the great mystery of which she was the minister: she kept them, waiting and learning during that long thirty years of silence, waiting and learning during that brief time of open labour, from the first words at the Marriage Feast to the last words from the Cross.   Luke i. 46 ff.   Luke ii.19.   Luke iii. 23.   John ii. 4 ; xix. 26.

And shall we, brethren, when we think on such an example, we with our restless and distracted lives, with our feeble and imperfect grasp on Truth, be contented to repeat with indolent assent a traditional confession ? Can we suppose that the highest knowledge, and the highest knowledge alone, is to be gained without effort, without

I. preparation, without discipline, and by a simple act of memory? Must the eye and the hand of the artist be trained through long years to discern and to portray subtle harmonies of form and colour, while that spiritual faculty by which we enter on the unseen may be safely left unexercised till some sudden emergency calls it into play? Is it credible that the law of our nature, which adds capacity to experience and joy to quest, is suddenly suspended when we reach the loftiest field of man's activity?

To ask such questions, as if the answer could be doubtful, is a reproach to our intelligence. To ask them in the silence of the soul, as seeking to feel their application, is a salutary discipline. We lose more than we know because we do not habitually meditate on the grandeur of our Creed. True it is that the vision which Plato imagined has been given to us as an abiding possession under the conditions of earth. But, that the divine revelation may become the master force of our whole being, we must dwell upon it. We must regard that most solemn Presence of the

John xiv. 9.

Father in Christ with lingering, loving, gaze till each detail grows significant to us according to the place which we occupy in the order of Providence. We must see it with our own eyes and not another's, thankful for every help to better in-

sight which we have inherited or enjoyed, but resting neither in the treasures of truth which we have
received nor in our own past gains.   The
sum of human experience grows visibly from age to
age ; the sum of personal experience grows visibly
from year to year ; and the Truth ought to find
fresh fulfilment in every fact of life.

In this respect we must, I fear, condemn ourselves of negligence.   For if, as I assume, the
Gospel touches us, yet we do not labour further to
trace the lines of its infinite expansion.   So it
comes to pass that we fail to gain a growing sense
of the obligations which it imposes, of the prerogatives which it confirms, of the strength which it
brings : strength, prerogatives, obligations, limited
only by our capacity to apprehend and appropriate
them, for *without controversy great is the mystery—*
the revelation—*of godliness*—not a formula or a
statement but a living Person, *even He Who was
manifested in the flesh, justified in the spirit, seen
of angels, preached among the nations, believed on
in the world, received up in glory.*

Yes : great, inexpressibly great, is *the mystery*
of our faith ; and at this season when the transcendent mystery, the transcendent revelation, is
once again specially brought before us, I desire, as
I may be enabled, to touch upon some points in
which it appears to me to concern us most nearly

I.

1 Tim. iii.
16.

I.   as men, as fallen men, as men placed in a world of marvellous complexity, as men busied with a life of endless issues ; to shew in other words a little more fully how, as indicated last summer, a patient contemplation of the Person and Work of Christ will enable us to meet with confidence and joy the trials of a new age.

But before we enter on the consideration of these four aspects of the Incarnation I wish by way of introduction to indicate now the spirit, the aim, the blessing of the work in which I invite you to help me by your thoughts, your sympathy, your prayers.

1.   The spirit.   In all that concerns the soul we know only when we love, and we know as we Hebr. xi. 6. love. *He who comes to God,* we read, *must believe that He is, and that He is a rewarder of them that diligently seek Him.* And more than this : he must believe that every thought of tender service and self-surrender, every aspiration towards a conscious fellowship with all created things, every striving towards a truer unity, by which we are stirred, corresponds in its essence with the infinite perfection of Him in Whose image we are made. He must interpret all that is noblest in the soul as a foreshadowing of Divine realities.   Thus Love springs out of Faith, Hebr. xi. 1. and is supported by it. Faith enables us to enter

on the unseen, to give reality to the fabrics of
hope. And Love, borne by faith, dimly sensible
of its power under the limitations of earth, rises
into that spiritual realm, and knows that all
things are possible to the love of GOD.

We shall then contemplate the signs of this
immeasurable love with the humblest reverence,
untroubled if we are unable to fit them together
perfectly under the forms of human thought. Nay
rather we shall rejoice that we cannot do so. Un-
reconciled antitheses are prophecies and promises
of a larger future: 'our failure is but a triumph's
evidence for the fulness of the days.' If
our Faith could find a complete and consistent
expression here it would be condemned. It
would not cover all the facts of life. The forms
of thought belong to this world only. The truth
of life, like man, like Christ Who is Himself
the Truth, belongs to two worlds. It is not
simply the determination of physical phenomena,
but the interpretation of the relation of man to
nature and to GOD. The heart has its own office
in the search for it. Not with the understanding, not with the reason, but with the heart
man believeth; and if ever our view becomes
clouded: if a thick darkness hides Him towards
Whom we strain our eyes: we shall recall for our
warning and for our chastening, humbled and yet

I.

Rom. x. 10.

sustained by hope, the benediction which tells us
that *the pure in heart shall see* GOD.

2.   This then will be our spirit, love illuminated by faith, attested by the heart.   And it
follows at once that our aim will be vital and
not merely intellectual.   We shall not strive to
gain any completeness of technical definition on
the doctrine of the Incarnation.   We acknowledge indeed that outlines are a necessity for
man's representation of the truth of things; but
they are a concession to his weakness and a
symbol of it.   There is no outline in nature, and
no form of words can adequately express a
spiritual reality.   The soul uses the outline, the formula, as an occasion, an impulse, a
help; but it brings from its own treasure that
which quickens them.   And in this work the soul
of the simplest, the most untutored, is at no dis-
advantage.   Its chief instrument of spiritual progress is not knowledge but love.

So we shall look upon the Incarnation, the
greatest conceivable thought, the greatest conceivable fact, not that we may bring it within the
range of our present powers, not that we may
measure it by standards of this world; but that we
may learn from it a little more of the awful
grandeur of life, that by its help we may behold
once again that halo of infinity about common

things which seems to have vanished away, that
thinking on the phrase *the Word became flesh* we
may feel that in, beneath, beyond, the objects
which we see and taste and handle is a Divine
Presence, that lifting up our eyes to the Lord in
glory we may know that phenomena are not ends,
but signs only of that which is spiritually dis-
cerned. And, while we confess that clearness of
vision cannot be gained when we turn towards
such an object except by the loss of that which is
characteristic of it—as we look at the sun shorn
of its glory through a darkened glass or through
the thick mists of earth—it will be our joy to
place ourselves in that atmosphere of light which
transfigures all that it falls upon.

3. This will be our aim; and no one can
have watched the tendencies of modern thought
without seeing that it answers to one of our sorest
needs. We are on the point of losing the sense of
the spiritual, the eternal, as a present reality, as
the only reality. Thought is not all: conduct is
not all: life is unspeakably impoverished if it is
unhallowed by the sanctities of reverence and
worship.

And, if we have felt one touch of the spirit
which should animate our contemplation of Christ
Born, Crucified, Ascended, for us; if we have
realised one least fragment of the end to which

I.
John i. 14.

I. our work is directed, we shall know what the
blessing is : know what it is to see with faint and
trembling eyes depth below depth opening in the
poor and dull surface of the earth ; to see flashes
of great hope shoot across the weary trivialities
of business and pleasure ; to see active about us,
in the face of every scheme of selfish ambition,
powers of the age to come ; to see in the struggles

Hebr. vi.
5.
of the forlorn and distressed fragments of the life
which 'the poor man' Christ Jesus lived ; to see
over all the inequalities of the world, its terrible
contrasts, its desolating crimes, its pride, its lust,
its cruelty, one overarching sign of GOD'S purpose

Gen. x. 13.
of redemption, broad as the sky and bright as the
sunshine ; to see in the Gospel a revelation of
love powerful even now to give a foretaste of the
unity of creation, powerful hereafter to realise it.

But, some will say, this blessing of faith,
even in its fullest power, still leaves unremoved
the evil, the sorrow, the suffering, the sin : the
sordid cares of want, the reckless indulgence of
wealth.   True : but it leaves them only
as one element in life, the most obvious, the most
oppressive, but not the most enduring or the most
powerful. It is when the physical order is held
to be all, that life appears and must appear to be
hopeless. As it is we can wait. We have found
GOD in the world; found Him not in an Eden from

which we are banished, but in our world, taking
to Himself our infirmities and sicknesses; and it
is enough to remember that we have found Him.
We see little; but He sees all.

I.
Matt. viii.
17.

We can therefore as we reflect on the Incarnation discern again 'the glory which hath passed
from earth' without disguising one dark trait.
We can recover with more than its first freshness
a sense of Divine beauty about us. And we need
the lesson in many ways. We need it, as I have
said, from the dominant forms of current thought,
and we need it from the conditions of life. As
years go on there is great danger lest we should
lose the ennobling faculty of wonder. We are
occupied with small cares and they become the
measure of our universe. Failures depress our
faith; and disappointments dull our hope. Then
this great spectacle of sovereign love rises before
us, and the common things of earth are again
touched with a heavenly light and become to us
figures of the divine. Then wonder grows with
knowledge; and though knowledge itself cannot
satisfy, it can lift the soul to GOD by disclosing
the infinite unknown.

At the same time the vision which elevates,
soothes and calms. Differences of earth vanish in
its presence. And if it be true that great duties
and little souls do not go well together; it is no

I.   less true that little thoughts do not suit little
duties. It is in the fulfilment of simple routine
that we need more than anywhere the quickening
influence of the highest thought; and this the
truth of the Incarnation, an eternal, an abiding
truth, is able to bring to every Christian. Life
may for a moment seem to be poor and mean and
commonplace, but, when the reflection of this
glory falls upon it, our wavering faith can alone
dim its brightness.

So it is that we gain the final sense of the
correspondence of the Gospel with the powers, the
circumstances, the needs of man: so we rejoice to
recognise the truth which we could not have
discovered: so we find that our human language
is not false, and our human aspirations are not
illusory: so we place over all that is fleeting in
form and transitory in its presentment the consecration of an eternal destiny.

The issue will not be gained at once. But
each effort to interpret the signs of the Divine
working will leave us stronger for new endeavours.
Each space of quiet thought will bring us power
of deeper vision. 'We have ourselves,' as it has
been well said, 'as we use ourselves.' And just as
our minds wither and waste if they are engrossed
by sordid cares, so the thought of GOD in Christ
enlarges and purifies every faculty which is

occupied with it, and lends something of its own   I.
nobility to the poorest heart which gives it a
welcome.

But we must never forget the inexorable law of
GOD's love. He gives *grace for grace.* He gives   John i. 16.
as His gifts are turned to service. He claims that
we should be His fellow-workers. We could   1 Cor. iii.
imagine no loftier title; and no lower title would   9.
answer to the purpose of our creation. We were
made to attain to the Divine likeness: made, that   Gen. i. 26.
is, as we can now see, to realise each in the narrow
sphere of our fragmentary lives, each according to
the measure of our ability, the fact of the Incarnation; to live in the light of that vision of
absolute truth which has been opened to us; to
live by the growth of that knowledge of GOD
which He places within our reach through the
fulfilment of daily duties.

To us also the Christ has been given.   Luke ii.
                                         11, 16, 19.
To us also the message of the angels has
been made known.

To us also the sign of the Saviour has been
fulfilled.

Happy are we—then only happy—if we
*keep all these things and ponder them in our
hearts.*

II.

THE INCARNATION AND THE CREATION.

[He] made known unto us the mystery of his will, according to his good pleasure which he purposed in him unto a dispensation of the fulness of the times, to sum up all things in Christ, the things in the heavens, and the things upon the earth. EPH. I. 9.

THE INCARNATION AND THE CREATION.

THE conception which we form of GOD necessarily determines the view which we form of
the world and of life.   This principle
holds true even when we recognise most fully that
our growing knowledge of the world and of life
quickens and enlarges our conception of GOD.
What then, we ask, characterises the Christian
conception of GOD ? To such a question we answer
at once that it is determined by the fact of the
Incarnation. *In the beginning was the Word, and*
the Word was with GOD, and the Word was GOD...
and the Word became flesh.   This great
mystery, this great revelation, is for us the *light*
in which we shall see light. It is evidently
inexhaustible in its teachings. It cannot be
completely interpreted by any one race, or by any
one age. As a fact of life it must become more
and more intelligible as experience and inquiry
reveal to us more completely the circumstances
and conditions of life. Each fresh result, won by

John i. 1,
14.

Ps. xxxvi.
9.

7—2

II. patient research into the constitution of our finite nature and of our sensible environment, helps us to understand a little better that truth which we have received, and therefore to apply it with a little greater force to the problems of the world.

In this respect it falls out that we can draw strength and instruction from our very trials. It is through difficulties fearlessly met that we are led to wider knowledge. We condemn ourselves to dead ignorance if we refuse to take account of them. In the order of Providence it comes to pass (may I not say it comes to pass by necessity?) that difficulties mark the direction of progress. It is obvious that the answer cannot be understood or effectively shaped till the question has been sharply put. A new requirement evokes unexpectedly a latent force. Hence it has happened in former times that the Truth has been found to satisfy needs which had made themselves felt in sadness and fear. The Faith which is in a Life, which is a Life, has been proved again and again to live itself, and to bring within its range larger fields of thought and larger promises of hope. And as it has been, so it will be still. The feelings, the desires, the movements of an age—of our own age—are not wholly in error. They are the manifestations,

often troubled and obscured by man's selfishness,   II.
of a Divine will.   Through these, as we believe,
GOD is leading us by His Spirit, sent in the Name   John xiv.
of His Son, to find a fuller meaning in the   26.
Creed which our fathers have transmitted to us to
use in the busy fields of action and not to hide in   Luke xix.
the barren security of a treasure-house.   20.

We inquire therefore without mistrust whether
there is any tendency of our own times which
seems likely to suggest to us fruitful questionings.   For my own part I find such a
tendency in that striving after some kind of
unity which has been stirred in many directions
by a novel sense of our connexion one with
another, and of our connexion with the material
world. No one can doubt the power of this
fascinating and generous impulse.   No one can
overlook its perils.   Influential teachers
persuade us on the one side to follow after the
unity of Naturalism, which limits all knowledge
to phenomena bound together by an inexorable
sequence : on the other side, to lull ourselves to
rest in the unity of Pantheism, which presents all
things indifferently as the manifestation of one
essence alone truly existent.

Such fictitious unities, however, can never bring
peace.   They take no account of our consciousness
of responsibility, incompleteness, disharmony :

II.   they take no real account of death.   But
if they are in themselves illusory, they do, I
believe, fulfil the office which I have assigned to
the spirit of the age.   They direct us to aspects of
the Incarnation which have not yet become the
heritage of the Church: to visions of great hope
through which we shall be enabled to meet the
temper of doubt among us, which is at once for-
midable by its sincerity and significant by its form.

They direct us, I repeat, to unrecognised
aspects of the Incarnation.   For it is no disloyalty
to the past to maintain that the view of the
Incarnation which was gained in the 4th or 5th
or 13th or 16th century was not final.   Our
fathers by the teaching of the Holy Spirit saw the
Truth, but they did not see all the Truth.   And
it is, I think, impossible to look at modern
writings without perceiving that the teaching on
Christ's Person which is current in the most
reverent schools falls short in many ways of the
living fulness of the Bible.   At one time
the logical development of His true divinity
leaves room only for a shadow of manhood, as
unsubstantial as the phantom which already
Hier. *Dial.* usurped His place when in a familiar phrase His
adv. Lcf. blood was still fresh in Palestine.   At
23. another time the loving portraiture of His true
humanity places Him before us as a man among

men, as one of many, as a part among parts; and   II.
not, according to His own self-chosen title, as the
Son of man in Whom all the separate endowments
of sex, and race and age co-exist in absolute
harmony.   In both ways we fail to grasp
the promise of unity which lies in the true view
of His Person. For in Holy Scripture He is
shewn to stand essentially in some ineffable yet
real connexion with all finite being. In Him, and Col. i. 16.
through Him, and unto Him were all things made.
He is the 'first-born,' 'the beginning' of all creation. Man was formed in His image; and in
Him men find their consummation.   The
forces of Nature, so to speak, are revealed to us in
the Bible as gathered together and crowned in
man, and the diversities of men as gathered
together and crowned in the Son of man; and so
we are encouraged to look forward to the end, to a
unity of which every imaginary unity on earth is
a phantom or a symbol, when the will of the
Father shall be accomplished and He shall *sum up*
all things in Christ—all things and not simply all Eph. i. 10.
persons—both *the things in the heavens and the*
things upon the earth.

If now we endeavour to determine the ultimate
cause of the defectiveness of the modern teaching
on the Person of Christ of which I have spoken,
we shall find it, I believe, most plainly shewn in

II.   the prevalent opinion as to the ground of the Incarnation. The Incarnation is commonly made to depend upon the Fall. And the whole tenour of revelation, as I conceive, leads us to regard the Incarnation as inherently involved in the Creation. The first Gospel is not the word of consolation: *The seed of the woman shall bruise the serpent's head,* but the word of the Divine counsel: *Let us make man in our image, after our likeness,* followed by the word of its initial accomplishment, *So GOD created man in His own image: in the image of GOD created He him.*

Gen. iii. 15.

Gen. i. 26, f.

In this august declaration of GOD'S purpose and GOD'S work we have set before us, clear beyond controversy, the primal endowment and the final goal of humanity. We are taught that man received, received inalienably as man, a fitness for gaining, through growth and discipline and continuous benediction, union with GOD. GOD'S image was given to him that he might gain GOD'S likeness. This original capacity of man was the measure of the love of GOD for His creature. Sin could not increase it: nothing less than personal union with GOD could fulfil it. The fitness and the necessity of the Incarnation exist therefore from the moment when man was made. The Incarnation, in other words, when we use the term in the most general sense,

apart from every thought of suffering and hu- II.
miliation, corresponds with the perfection of man
as he was constituted at first, and not merely
with the restoration of man who had missed his
end. *Homo particeps Dei*—Man made partaker
of GOD—is the satisfaction, the only possible
satisfaction, of *Homo capax Dei*—Man capable of
receiving GOD. The marvel is that the purpose of
creation was wrought out in spite of that wilful
self-assertion of the creature which might have
seemed to have fatally thwarted it.

Brethren, if you have in any degree followed
me—and the thoughts which I have desired to
suggest are rather strange and unfamiliar than
intrinsically difficult—if you have felt, however
dimly, what this Gospel of Creation is, I do not
fear that you will think that I have directed your
attention to fantastic or idle speculations. When a
thousand hearts wait for some voice of encouragement, who would dare to beguile them with subtle
fancies? Nay, rather, it is because the truth on
which I have touched, the truth on which I pray
you to meditate, seems to me to be intensely
practical that I have striven to set it before you.
For me at least the thought of the predestined
humanity of the Eternal Word, the Son of GOD, as
the archetype of humanity, throws light, growing
light, upon some of those points of the Faith,

II. where many of us feel the darkness to be most oppressive.

It throws light upon the most solemn mystery of the Being of GOD. It helps us to understand how finite being was so ordered as to convey to a creature formed in the image of GOD a knowledge of GOD's nature and will, and thus to fit him to become a living and conscious shrine of His glory. It keeps GOD near to us in the fulness of our whole constitution. It teaches us to welcome and to use the imperfect conclusions of that Naturalism which offers a partial homage to the majestic progress of the physical order. It confirms the splendid visions which lend an unreal beauty to Pantheism by pointing to the

1 Cor. xv. 28. end when *GOD shall be all in all.*

It throws light upon the broken and chequered sum of human existence. It helps us to understand how the scattered fragments in which man's potential endowments have hitherto been realised combine to form a whole. There is a law, there is a Head from the first. There is no absolute separation of men in the complex variety of their functions. Men, so to speak, furnish the manifold elements through which (in the language

Eph. i. 23. of St Paul) a body of Christ is shaped; just as the world furnishes the elements through which man himself finds expression for his character.

It throws light on the conception of personality.   ii.
It helps us to understand how the self-assertion of
the finite is sin and death; and how the complete
self-surrender of love preserves and fulfils that which
is truly individual, by delivering it from the weakness of isolation, by consecrating it to common
service, by incorporating it in Him Who is *the* John xiv.
Life.   Thus directed we can see that all ⁶·
the differences of men, so far as they correspond
with a true growth, contribute to the manifestation of the infinite perfection of the Son
of man.

It throws light upon the connexion of man and
nature. It helps us to understand how every
discovery which encourages us to see an order in
the unfolding of all things confirms the teaching
of revelation on the Divine method and the
Divine end : how the division, the differentiation
of parts—call it as we will,—which culminates in
man, points forward to a unity as well as backward :
how the restoration of unity to mankind carries
with it the restoration of unity to finite being.

It throws light, yet once again, upon the
mystery of the future. It helps us to understand
how that existence to which we look in hope is
not a mere indefinite continuance of divided lives,
in which each one dwells apart, but some higher
type of a common life : a life in Christ : a life felt Gal. iii.
28.

II. in the fulness of personal fruition to be His life to which all in due measure offer that which is theirs: a life which thrills through each least member of the spiritual body with the intense and untiring joy of an absolute harmony.

It throws light, as I hope to shew next Sunday, upon the deep truths of the Atonement, upon the fulfilment of the destiny of man fallen. But not to enter on this subject now, I cannot but think that the idea of 'the Gospel of Creation' has already been shewn to be fruitful in great thoughts in relation to man as he was made by GOD. We welcome it, we keep it in our hearts, we ponder it; and little by little there takes shape before us a vision of the unity of nature in man, and of the unity of men in Christ, which satisfies desires that at present shew themselves importunately urgent. As we look and look, sending our souls with unwearied, unsatisfied delight through the infinities of time and space, there is, if I may so express myself, offered for our contemplation first an unfolding through the Divine creative love, and then an ingathering, an infolding, through the Divine perfective (or, as it is in fact, redemptive) love. We see, inscribed upon the age-long annals in which the prophetic history of the world and of humanity has been written, the sentence of inextinguishable hope, 'From

Rom. xi. 36.

GOD unto GOD.' We see when we look back upon
the manifestation of the Divine plan that the
order which we trace—nature, humanity, Christ—
corresponds inversely with our earnest expectation of its fulfilment—Christ, the sons of GOD,
nature.   We see, in short, while we thus
regard the universe, as we must do, under the
limitation of succession, from first to last a
supreme harmony underlying all things which
even sin cannot destroy.   As yet, it is true, *we see
only in part, through a glass, in a riddle,* but
under this aspect we do see enough to make
labour hopeful, to make thought consistent, and
to bring every object which we perceive or feel
within the scope of love.

   How can it be otherwise ?   We all know how
the astronomers of the middle ages were baffled
by continually increasing perplexities as long as
they endeavoured to refer the motions of the
heavenly bodies to a central earth.   When once
the sun was taken for the centre all became
clear, and the irregularities which remained have
been the fertile source of later discoveries.   So it
is with Theology.   Looking to the Incarnation as
the crown of Creation we have found the true
centre of the system in which we are set to work,
even GOD and not man, love and not sin, the
Creation which was the expression of the Father's

II.

Rom. viii.
18 ff.

1 Cor. xiii.
12.

II. will, and not the Fall which was alien from it.   Under the action of that central force of the Divine love the Incarnation reveals to us the essential possibilities and endowments of each separate life.   It lifts us out of ourselves, above ourselves, that so we may find our truest selves in Him, Who has come to us that we may Col. i. 16. come to Him, for Whom we were made and Who for us *became flesh.*   In this double truth, which is one truth, we have in the face of things seen and temporal the test and the pledge of the eternal.   All that truly *is* is the gift of God, summed up in His first and last gift of Himself.

With bowed heads and open hearts may we offer ourselves—we can do no more and we dare do no less—to the action of His love in and for which He created us.   For us the nobility of freedom lies in the sense of dependence.   For us the fulness of strength lies in the simplicity of Faith.   We gaze for an instant on the Majesty within the veil that we may go forth Ps. civ. 23. again into the world, *to our work and to our labour,* and still bear about with us the strong Heb. vi. 5; assurance that the powers of the heavenly order xii. 2. are placed within our reach : that above the clouds and darkness which beset our path He is throned Who has borne our nature to the right hand of

GOD : that *in many parts and in many fashions,* through sufferings and chastisements, the Divine purpose is being fulfilled : that behind the veils of sense, which perplex and distract us, burns the serene glory of the Divine Presence : that beyond the spectacle of failures and conflicts which flow from selfishness, glows the prospect of a holy unity passing knowledge—a holy unity which shall here- after crown and fulfil creation as one revelation of Infinite Love, when the Father's will is accom- plished and He has *summed up all things in Christ, the things in the heavens and the things upon earth.*

II.
Heb. i. 1.

III.

THE INCARNATION AND THE FALL.

*It was the good pleasure of the Father that in Him
should all the fulness dwell ; and through Him to reconcile
all things unto Himself, having made peace through the
blood of His Cross ; through Him, I say, whether things upon
the earth, or things in the heavens.*

COL. I. 19, 20.

THE INCARNATION AND THE FALL.

WE have seen already that the Divine record of Creation is indeed a Gospel, a revelation of the purpose of GOD'S love for humanity. We have seen that the order of finite being is, as it is made known to us, fitted to be a manifestation of points in the character of GOD, leading up to the manifestation of Himself. We have seen that man was made capable of union with GOD, and that the possession of that capacity as a Divine endowment implies a promise of its satisfaction. We have seen that if, with our weak and disordered powers, we endeavour now to imagine what would have been the normal course of unfallen humanity towards its glorious goal, we must think of the happy and complete realisation of every potential energy of our nature through the discipline of a life relatively perfect, though fragmentary; for so the Divine likeness would have found fulfilment in

8—2

III.
many parts: so at last the parts would have found unity in Him in Whose image man was made. We have seen that the conceivableness of the Incarnation lies in the thought of what man was originally made, and not in what he became through his self-assertion. We have seen that this Gospel of Creation is able to illuminate dark mysteries of the present and of the future, to disclose new depths for our contemplation in the nature of GOD and in the nature of man, to open dim foregleams of a unity which passes all understanding.

But while our eyes rest on the splendid vision, we are forced to ask whether it is indeed for us: whether we have not lost our birthright and our blessing beyond recall: whether the destiny of man can still be accomplished when he instinctively shrinks from Him in Whose Presence is life?

We all, I say, ask such questions when we regard the contradictions in our souls.

For everyone recognises in himself the two conflicting truths which are expressed in the narrative of the Fall: the power of evil and the prerogative of personal responsibility. There is we feel a 'baseness in our blood,' and we feel also that we have embodied the corruption 'by our fault, by our own fault, by our own great fault.'

The tendency indeed is our inheritance, but we have made the issues our own by deed; we are actually, and we know ourselves to be, guilty, enthralled, alienated from GOD.   We look around us, and we see the double sentence of our own consciences written on a larger scale in the crimes and judgments of classes and nations, in the deeds of selfish violence which betray a common taint, and in the clear, unquestioning appeal of suffering souls to the majesty of a violated law.

What shall we say then? Is there for sinful men, for sinful humanity, forgiveness, redemption, reconciliation: a forgiveness which not only remits the debt, but also removes the consequences which the debt has impressed upon the character: a redemption which not only rescues the captive from his oppressor, but also inspires him with the vigour of freedom: a reconciliation which not only withdraws the barrier against the outflow of the love of GOD, but also opens the frozen springs of love in man? Or, is the evil which we see and feel irremediable?

We have heard indeed and we have dwelt with wonder on the primal purpose of GOD *to sum up all things in Christ.* But is that all? if so, we ask again, how can this purpose apply to us, being what we are?   St Paul seems to have

III.

Eph. i. 10.

III.   asked himself the same question; and he has
           answered it for us. *It was,* he says, *the good*
Col. i. 19 f. *pleasure of the Father through* [*The Son of His Love*]
           to reconcile all things unto Himself, having made
           peace through the blood of His cross. It was the
           purpose of GOD 'to reconcile' and not only 'to
           sum up'; 'to reconcile all things through Christ',
           by the efficacy of His action, and not only 'to sum
           up all things in Christ' by the embracing energy
           of His Nature; to *make peace* where confusion
           and conflict had found entrance; *to make peace*
           by blood, by the outpouring of a consecrated life
           given for the life of the world.   Sin, in
           other words, did not alter the Divine purpose,
           but it modified the mode of its fulfilment.

              In part we can understand this. Man did not
Gen. ix. 9. lose the image of GOD by the Fall. His essential
           nature still remained capable of union with GOD,
           but it was burdened and hampered. The Word
           therefore could still become flesh, but if in His
           infinite compassion He was pleased to realise this
           fellowship of the Divine and human, He took to
           Himself naturally, if we may so speak, humanity
           with its immeasurable obligations, life with its
           untold temptations and sorrows.   In this
           there is nothing arbitrary, nothing which is not
           illustrated by universal experience, nothing which
           is not in accordance with the actual constitution

of the world. By becoming man the Word ac- III.
cepted the uttermost consequences of human existence : by becoming the Son of man, the Head, the
representative of the race, He embraced them in
their widest range.

In part, I repeat, we can understand this. We
can understand how Christ—the Word become
flesh—could suffer.

But some one will say, 'True : but if we allow
that Christ could and did suffer : if we allow that
men are bound one to another by the consequences
of descent and the effects of intercourse : that
they were so made as to rejoice and to weep
together : that this is true socially and individually,
true of states and of citizens : if we allow that
Christ, by becoming man, entered on the accumulated heritage of human woes of His own will;
yet my chief difficulty is untouched. How can
another's suffering avail for my offence ? How
can punishment be at once vicarious and just?'
And perhaps he will add, 'I fairly claim an
answer to my question. GOD did not refuse to
accept the pleading of Abraham, which was based
upon the human apprehension of righteousness;
and He will not refuse to listen to our inquiry
to-day; when we too say, *Shall not the Judge of all* Gen. xviii.
the earth do right ?' 25.

Yes, brethren, I at once admit that this, which

III.

is indeed the question of questions for us, ought to be met. And when I said last Sunday that it is through our difficulties honestly stated and faced that GOD is pleased to guide us to fuller truth: when I said that under this aspect the characteristic thoughts of an age become articulate voices through the living interpretation of the Spirit: I was thinking not least of this question. For of all the directions in which the tendency towards unity, of which I spoke, has found expression, that which has led to the apprehension of social unity is perhaps the most fertile in suggestions for our own needs. Fifty years ago the term 'solidarity' and the idea which it conveys were alike strange or unknown. We had not apprehended in any living way that we are, as St Paul

Rom. xii. 5.

says, literally *members one of another*, as men and nations. It was then fashionable to regard a state as an aggregation of individuals bound together by considerations of interest or pleasure. But we have now learnt in some degree, and we are learning better from year to year, that the family and not the individual is the unit of human life: that the nation is a larger family: that humanity is the ultimate family: that, in all these, the fundamental relations represented by parents, brothers and sisters, children, repeat themselves on different scales and offer final types

of order and progress: that we and our fathers and   III.
our posterity have been and must be born sons
and citizens, heirs and stewards of wealth, physical,
moral, spiritual, which no isolated effort could
have accumulated: that the family, the nation,
the race, are living wholes which cannot be broken
up by any effort of individual will.   We
have learnt, in some degree, and we are learning
better from year to year, to keep at the same time
the humblest sense of our dependence and the
liveliest sense of our liberty: to realise as a moral
power the feeling of the unbroken continuity of
life through the past and the present and the
future: to acknowledge not only the necessity but
also the blessing of suffering for others: to feel
that St Paul has revealed the power and the
limit of sympathy when he tells us in the same
paragraph: *Bear ye one another's burdens...and* Gal. vi.
each man shall bear his own load. Yes: love can 2, 5.
lighten the weight of the suffering which it cannot remove: it can transform what it cannot
destroy.   We have learnt, that is, in some
degree, and are learning better from year to year,
the one thought which, as far as I can see, makes
it possible to believe the Gospel in its fulness, and
not to close the eyes upon the facts of the world,
the miseries of an African war, the burden of an
Indian Empire.

III.   Taught in this great school of domestic,
national, human fellowship, we are coming to
understand, as we could not do before, that sin
affects not the individual only but the race, and
that the just consequences of sin in every form
answer to a law of holy love ; that they include, as
we regard them in parts, the ideas of reparation,
of chastisement, of cleansing, which to our eyes
are realised in parts slowly and in unexpected
ways : to understand that in the conduct of our
disordered life suffering contributes to the hallowing of man and of men : to understand that to
noble and pure souls some imperfect yet real
power of restoration is given, proportioned to
their knowledge and their sympathy, and their
Hebr. v. 2. holiness—to their capacity for entering into the
hearts of the ignorant, the weak and the erring,
and for calling out in them the response of penitent devotion : to understand that in the unity of
Matt. viii. the body it is possible for one member to take
17.   away the infirmity and disease of another by taking
them to himself.

Taught in this great school we are coming to
understand why the human instinct has always
rejoiced in the stories of uncalculating self-devotion
which brighten the annals of every people : why
our hearts respond to the words of a Chinese king,
contemporary with Jacob, who said to his people,

'When guilt is found anywhere in you who occupy 'the myriad regions, let it rest on me the One 'man'; and faithful to his prayer said again, when a human victim was demanded to avert a drought, 'If a man must be the victim, I will be he:[1]' why we do not think lives wasted which are offered in heroic prodigality to witness to a great principle: why the blood of martyrs is indeed seed, not idly spilt upon the ground, but made the vital source of a teeming harvest: we are coming to understand, in a word, what is the true meaning of that phrase 'vicarious suffering' which has brought at other times sad perplexity to anxious minds; how it excludes everything that is arbitrary, fictitious, unnatural, external in human relationships; how it expresses the highest energy of love which takes a friend's sorrows into the loving heart and taking them by GOD'S grace transfigures them, satisfying every claim of righteousness, justifying every instinct of hope, quickening the spirit of self-surrender, offering within the sphere of common life a faint image of forgiveness, of redemption, of reconciliation.

So we are brought back to our great question, Can there be just forgiveness, redemption, reconciliation for sin? So I think we are prepared to

---

[1] Sacred Books of the East: *The Shu king: The announcement of Thang*, p. 91, and note.

III.   answer it.   We have found that the idea of the
unity of humanity which underlies the Bible is
brought home to us in daily intercourse : we have
found that 'suffering is the fuel of love', the means
of its perfecting, purifying action alike on him
who suffers and on him for whom the suffering is
borne : we have found that the measure of love's
restorative efficacy in common human intercourse
lies in knowledge, sympathy, holiness.   Let
then the knowledge be complete : let the sympathy
reach to every creature : let the holiness be absolute : and there is provision for the atonement of
fallen humanity ; there is a propitiation for sins
co-extensive with their presence ; there is a force
of all most prevailing to kindle the activity of
Faith.

Each of these conditions was satisfied when *the*
John i. 14. *Word became flesh* ; and now we can see how the
Gospel of Creation meets our misgivings.   Christ
the Son of GOD, the Son of man, took to Himself a nature which from the first it was His
good pleasure to crown.   In Him every scattered
fragment of manhood found its proper Head.   Not
one wrong through all its sad development was
outside His penetrating knowledge.   Not one
least sorrow was alien from His spontaneous
sympathy.   Not one proud boast of self-sufficiency
could maintain itself in the burning light of His

holiness. In Him men were able to recognise the III.
harmonious maturity of every human endowment.
In Him each man was able to recognise the
consecration of his peculiar gift. In Him every
single personality finds its true self.

Thus we can see, even if it be in a riddle,
a little more of the meaning of the Incarnation. Christ fulfilled perfectly the destiny
of man, fulfilled through suffering the destiny of
man fallen, realising at every stage and through
death itself union with GOD: there lies for the
whole race in Him the promise of forgiveness. Christ bore to the uttermost, even
to the Cross, the consequences of human sin, and
gave His blood to men as the power of a new life:
there lies for the whole race the means of redemption. Christ shewed the Father's love
with such persuasiveness of tender mercy as to
move every awakened conscience to glad self-surrender: there lies for the whole race the potency of
reconciliation.

And in all this there is nothing which offends
the most delicate susceptibility of natural right- Heb. ii. 10
eousness; nothing which does not find an antici- $(\check{\epsilon}\pi\rho\epsilon\pi\epsilon\nu)$.
patory welcome in the homage which is joyously
rendered to self-sacrifice; nothing which does not
find prophetic foreshadowing in the beneficent
influence which the devotion of one man exer-

III.

cises over the hearts of others, to inspire and to chasten.

Now therefore at last we can see how the mystery of Redemption corresponds to the mystery of the Fall. *If by the trespass of the one the many died, much more—'* much *more'—did the grace of God and the gift by the grace of the one man Jesus Christ abound unto the many.* On the one side we deplore our corruption, and we confess our guilt. On the other side we see in Christ the perfection of that towards which we strain, a perfection which He offers to us. God grant that we may take it by the faith which realises our fellowship with him. For forgiveness, redemption, reconciliation, are not blessings which Christ bestows apart from Himself, but in Himself: in the humanity which He has created afresh and cleanses by His blood.

Rom. v. 15.

Oh, my friends, what an inexhaustible motive for labour lies in the revelation of one humanity, one in Creation, one in Redemption, one potentially in Christ. We cannot, if we would, gain our happiness alone: we cannot be saved alone. There is a wonderful Indian legend which tells how a Buddhist saint had reached by successive lives of sacrifice the stage next to Nirvâna. At that point he could by one effort

III.

of will obtain for himself eternal and untroubled calm. But when the decision had to be made he set aside the tempting prize, and chose rather to live again in the world while conflict could bear fruit. 'Not,' he said, 'till the last soul on every earth and in every hell has found peace can I enter on my rest.'

Do we not feel the Christian truth, which is enshrined in the splendid story? Not for ourselves only, as some peculiar and private blessing, is the Gospel given, the Gospel of Creation, the Gospel of the Word Incarnate. It is for the world; and it is laid upon us, upon each one of us, to realise what Christ has wrought for men, to claim for Him the fruits of His victory. We look upon the terrible spectacle of remediable evils thronging about us on every side: we look upon the Cross which has been made before our eyes an altar and a throne: we look upon the apostolic words which interpret the Father's purpose *to reconcile all things unto Himself through the Son of His love.* And our hearts accept the message of the will of GOD, as when from the great host at Clermont one voice welcomed the call to the first Crusade, and we too say, welcoming the call to fulfil Christ's triumph, 'It is the will of GOD.' That old call was to win by force of arms, through violence and desolation and slaughter, an

John xvi. 33.

Gal. iii. 1; Heb. xiii. 10; John xii. 32.

III.　empty sepulchre : the call which we hear is to win
by patience and love, through self-devotion and
sacrifice, the living Body of Christ, the Church of
Acts xx.　redeemed humanity which He has *purchased*
28.　*with His own blood.*　　　'Deus vult ! Deus
vult.'　'It is the will of God.'

IV.

THE INCARNATION AND NATURE.

For the earnest expectation of the creation waiteth for the revealing of the sons of GOD....For we know that the whole creation groaneth and travaileth in pain together until now.

ROM. VIII. 19, 22.

THE INCARNATION AND NATURE.

IT was my object last Sunday to shew how one of the most characteristic thoughts of our age, that of the living membership of man with man and of nation with nation, the thought of the solidarity of humanity, which we have ourselves seen to take shape among us and to enter into popular aspirations, illuminates two of the greatest mysteries of our Faith, the mystery of the Fall and the mystery of the Atonement: how it throws light upon the meaning of suffering and upon the power of love: how it reconciles the instinct which affirms the absolute supremacy of righteousness, and the instinct which rejoices in the triumphs of self-devotion: how it gives to us in a form which the heart can embrace that conception of a common human life, in which the sense of corruption and the sense of responsibility, the acknowledgment of the fulfilment of man's

9—2

IV.   destiny and the power of personally appropriating
the virtue of Christ's work, are brought together
in a vital harmony : how it offers to us a motive
for labour which is able to consecrate every faculty
and a spring of encouragement which is sufficient
to refresh every fainting heart : how it inspires us
to write over the wavering expression of the
noblest ambition by which we have ever been
stirred, of the loftiest hope to which we have ever
reached forward, the sentence of Divine assurance,
'It is the will of GOD.'

All this seems to me to follow, to follow necessarily, from bringing the truth of the union
of man with man, which great modern teachers
have made known to us, into connexion with the
central fact of the Incarnation.   But the
same masters have taught us also another truth.
They have enabled us to realise, with a vividness
impossible in earlier times, not only our union one
with another but also our common union with nature.   By this work they have doubled our
debt to them, though for a time they seemed to
have effaced the landmarks of man's heritage.
They have in the end moved us to enter with
surer trust a little further into the depths of
the Scriptural doctrine of Creation, to welcome
as sober truth the language which claims the
Ps. cxlviii.
9.   service of life from *mountains and all hills,*

fruitful trees and all cedars, to find that in all
that is truly human, in all that is eternal, the
thoughts of the written Word, if we go back to it
with faithful, loving, humble, hearts, are ever
beyond and before us, quickening us with grander
aspirations, strengthening us with larger hopes,
embracing in their wider range the last results
which have been won by others from the study of
the world.

Man then, I assume, is bound as closely on
one side to earth and the creatures of earth as he
is bound on the other side to heaven. So he
appears in the Bible as the crown and king of
Nature. He is neither above nor separated from
the other works of GOD. Like a true king he
delights in fellowship with his subjects. His
isolation from the realm committed to him is a
doctrine of heathen philosophy and not of
Judaism or of Christianity. In revelation
no less than in science man is the representative
of Creation, who gathers up into himself and
combines in the most perfect form the various
manifestations of life and being which are seen
dispersed tentatively, as it were, through other
orders.

This fact, when once it is admitted, can be
used and has been used in two opposite ways.
Some have found in it the occasion for degrading

IV.

man to the level of their superficial estimate of the material world. Others, with a wider hope, have seen in the relation of matter to man indications, prophecies, promises, of some larger life than we have yet been able to conceive.

There can be no doubt to which alternative observation and inquiry are rapidly converging. 'Under one of its aspects,' writes Mr Herbert Spencer in his most recent volume, 'scientific progress is a gradual transfiguration of Nature. Where ordinary perception saw perfect simplicity it reveals great complexity; where there appeared absolute inertness it discloses intense activity; and in what appears mere vacancy it finds a marvellous play of forces...The conception to which [the explorer of Nature] tends is much less that of a Universe of dead matter than that of a Universe everywhere alive...'

Such a calm and solemn summary of the latest results of unbiassed research helps us, I repeat, to understand the words of St Paul in which he tells us that *the earnest expectation of the Creation waiteth for the revealing of the sons of GOD...for we know that the whole Creation groaneth and travaileth in pain together until now,* words which stand alone in the Bible as a plain enunciation of facts of overwhelming magnificence: words which now at length are becoming in-

Rom. viii. 19.

telligible to us in their vast import : words which
distinctly lay down as elements of our spiritual
consolation the dependence of Creation upon man
both in his fall and in his restoration, the vital
unity of the whole visible order which we are at
present able to contemplate, the Divine law of
progress by which all that is imperfect moves
towards a second birth.

The expression of these truths is indeed, as I
have said, unique, but the truths themselves fall
in with the entire scope of Scripture ; and the first
lesson this afternoon (Is. lxv.) has reminded us
that the renovation of the world forms as con-
spicuous a subject of the prophetic gospel as the
renovation of society.   It could not be otherwise ;
for the sympathy of Nature with man is written
on the first page of the Bible and on the last.   In
the spiritual history of Genesis the earth is said Gen. iii.
to have been cursed for man's sake.   In the 17.
spiritual vision of the Apocalypse new heavens Apoc. xxi.
and a new earth are prepared for redeemed 1.
humanity.   Meanwhile the necessity of anxious
toil, imposed upon us by the conditions of life in
this season of our conflict, is designed by a
Father's love for salutary discipline ; and on the
other hand we are encouraged to believe that *the
earnest expectation of the Creation waiteth for the
revealing of the sons of GOD*, waiteth, in due season,

to reflect their glory even as they will reflect the glory of their Saviour at His Coming: waiteth, and yet not in mere idle and passive expectancy, but to receive a blessing towards which it has striven through a discipline of fruitful suffering. *For the whole Creation groaneth and travaileth in pain together until now.*

The whole Creation groaneth and travaileth in pain together until now. Not at once, and, in their fulness, not at last, can we grasp the teaching of these wonderful words. But three points are sufficiently clear in them. They set before us the thoughts of a common life in Creation, of a life of pain, of a life of pain leading to a new birth.

1. There is a common life in Creation. Our own little life is for each one of us of such absorbing interest that we often use it to measure the idea of life itself. We can apply the standard successfully to those forms of life with which we are most familiar and which we can readily embrace in what appears to be their completeness. But, as we have already seen, the life of a nation, the life of humanity, the life of the Body of Christ, transcends its application. And now St Paul carries us beyond the ultimate societies of men. He leads us to see the functions of a common life in all Nature, in things irrational, and in things, as we speak, inanimate. He bids

us regard them as truly united in the circumstances of their present condition and of their
future consummation.

We observe so little and for so short a time:
the play of forces around us is so complicated and
so distracting : our point of sight is so completely
immersed in the movement which we wish to
calculate ; that it is hopeless for us to seek for
more than a dim sense of the immeasurable life
which is thus suggested. But that sense alone,
vague and fleeting as it may be, is inestimably
precious.   He who has gained it, he who
has gained it and used it to give reality to his
belief that it was the good pleasure of GOD *to sum*
up all things in Christ, the things in the heavens
and the things upon the earth, has gained that
which is able to transfigure the aspect of the
world.

2. For this life of the Universe is for the
present manifested to us in pain. *The whole Cre-*
ation groaneth together. Through all its parts
there are to our sight marks of failure, of
imperfection, of suffering ; and these St Paul
describes in the language of consciousness because
that in which they are found is a living whole;
and man cannot but express ideas of life in terms
of his own life.   But the language is no
utterance, as has been most falsely said, of a

IV.

Eph. i. 10.

IV.   'pathetic fallacy.' It witnesses with commanding
power, even in its sadness, to that kinsmanship of
being which lies in a common divine origin. 'A
world which GOD made dead?' Nay rather,
death comes from sin, and we communicate the
semblance of our deadness to our environment.

We communicate to our environment the semblance of our deadness, as we have communicated
to it once for all the issues of our Fall. For no
one, I suppose, can fail to have been struck with the
inexpressibly sombre aspect which nature offers to
our human sight. There is, as it must seem, a
prodigal waste of life. A gust of wind sweeping
along an avenue scatters over the ground seeds
which might give birth to a forest, and not one of
them is fruitful.   There is a fierce struggle
for existence, type against type, class against class,
unit against unit; and the balance of parts in the
organisation of life is so delicate that a small
change in one of them is sufficient to bring
destruction to a whole race.   There is the
inherent incompleteness of life, which is such that
no individual ever reaches the full measure of
its characteristic energy or beauty. Everywhere
we seem to read the same sad tale. Thousands
are sacrificed to one; and that one fails.

3. It would be easy to pursue in detail the
terrible indictment: easy to shew that, if, according

to the beautiful Greek fancy, the clay of which
man was moulded was moistened not with water
but with tears, every strain of natural music as it
strikes upon our senses dies away into a dirge:
easy to paint the ashy tint of death which follows
the glow of burning purple on the mountain side
when the sun has set: easy to round all in gloom,
if we pause in our first experience. But we may
not pause here. St Paul recognises the
deep voice of grief in the Creation but he does not
rest in it. *The whole Creation,* he says, *groaneth
and travaileth together until now.* The sorrow is
unto joy at last. Out of that which appears to us
to be a confused struggle shall come a new and
more perfect life. The pains which we witness
are the very conditions of the birth of the new
order. In this case also, as with man, the
passage to life is through suffering. But we
believe that not one agony is wasted, and in part
we can justify our faith. The same facts which
are full of sadness when referred to the individual are full of hope when referred to the
whole. Constant rivalry under the actual conditions of earth—conditions which express the
will of GOD—provides for a gradual eleva-
tion of type, and in the long run that form
survives which is best fitted for the work to be
done. Under this aspect the largest

John xvi. 21.

IV.   lessons of human life are reassuring. Races, king-
doms, societies, like individuals, pass away when
they have fulfilled their part. They pass away,
and yet they live on in the greater order which
they have prepared; so that we already rejoice in
the assurance that descendants better and nobler
than ourselves will carry on and perfect that
which we have rudely prepared.   Nor do
we stay here. We are constrained to think that
this joy may find a place also in the larger realm
of Nature. The prospect may be obscure in the
present, from the imperfection of our powers, but
at least what we do see justifies the picture which
we draw. As far as we can look back the earth
was slowly prepared through many changes, by fire
and frost, by flood and earthquake, to be the scene
of man's discipline; and since the time came
for man to enter on his kingdom, his advance
may fairly be taken as the measure of advance in
all below him.

So far Nature alone guides us with lights
fitful and scattered, yet kindled at a heavenly
source. But now let the thought of the Incarnation come in, the thought that it was the Father's
good pleasure from the first to rear through the
ages a living shrine for His Word which became
conscious in man: the thought that the eternal
Son has taken to Himself the firstfruits of our

terrestrial order in His Body through the grave to
the throne of GOD: the thought that as *in Him
were all things created* so *in Him all things consist,*
and it is for us, I will dare to say, a new creation
of the world.　　　Every token of inner and
manifold life in *all things in the heavens and
upon the earth* assumes a fresh significance.
The seed wasted, the feebler being swept away,
the effort marred, have each their proper value and
contribute to the fulness of the whole.　　　In
the tender love of that all-embracing Presence
every unit stands out in clear distinctness from
the innumerable host in which its sensible action
is absorbed. The limits of the activity of finite
being are not circumscribed by human experience. The world is not a great museum of
specimens to be arranged with exhaustive knowledge, but a revelation of life, where knowledge
is the herald of reverence and the minister of
love.　　　The progress of the past is the
sign and not the measure of that which shall
be when the glory of the sons of GOD shall be
reflected by the scene of their finished labour;
or rather when we, with pure and opened eyes,
shall see the world as GOD made it.

> "O world, as GOD has made it! All is beauty:
> And knowing this is love, and love is duty.
> What further may be sought for, or declared?"

IV.   For even now, as I must think, faint, fragmentary traces of the splendid vision are being
disclosed to us.   There is (who does not know it?)
much in the peculiar circumstances of our life and
thought to disquiet and distress, but there is
much also, much which is offered to us first by
the Spirit of GOD, to compensate and calm our
anxieties; much above all in those larger views of
life which tend to make the fact of the Incarnation, I will venture to say, the most natural of all
facts.

It may be that in our day of trial we shall
fail to apprehend the new messages of widening
wisdom : that we shall cling blindly to fixed
traditional forms of opinion which do not correspond with the requirements of our spiritual
position : that we shall seek to confine within
artificial limits, through timorous distrust, that
which is a power of infinite growth.

It may be : but innumerable voices fill us
with a better hope.   As yet indeed they are not
blended into one prayer, one confession, one
thanksgiving.   But beneath their accidental and
temporary discordances there is one ruling thought
expressed in many ways, now with trembling
pathos and now with unchastened boldness, the
thought of one life, one Spirit, one Lord and
Saviour, one GOD and Father of all.   And

the Gospel of Creation fulfilled in the Gospel of   IV.
the Word made flesh is able to unite them.   Not
one secret won from Nature by unconscious
interpreters of the Divine will, not one fact
shewn to have been realised in history by the
students of human progress, not one cry of
penitence, or one aspiration of faith, which rises
from the solitary soul, fails to find a place in the
majestic range of that Gospel, fails, if we look
aright, to shew it in more sovereign grace.

The characteristic sign of the Messianic Presence on which the prophets dwelt, was 'the Is. xxxv.
opening of the eyes of the blind': so may GOD in 5.
His mercy open *the eyes of our hearts* that we Eph. i. 18.
may behold the King Who comes to us in His Is. xxxiii.
beauty.   More hangs upon our faith than mind 17.
can imagine or embrace.   The work which through
our ministry embodies the grace of Christ
affects, by His will, not ourselves only, not our
fellow-men only, but all things in heaven and on
earth, all things which He has made as the image
of His love.   Even now, in the sight of our overmastering self-absorption, our faint endeavours,
*the earnest expectation of the Creation waiteth for
the revealing of the Sons of GOD.*

V.

THE INCARNATION AND LIFE.

For of his fulness we all received, and grace for grace.

ST JOHN I. 16.

THE INCARNATION AND LIFE.

WE have hitherto considered the Incarnation in relation to the widest thoughts of life and being, as the crown of the original purpose of Creation, as the fulfilment of the destiny of man in spite of sin, the fruit of self-assertion, as the revelation of the vital unity of Nature. The vision which is thus opened to devout contemplation is of such transcending splendour that there is a danger lest we should allow ourselves to be occupied with it, to be absorbed by it, to be lost in it, as it were, in a kind of indolent optimism. We are tempted to say when we gain a faint impression of the magnificent range of the divine order, and of the unexpected ways in which the divine counsel is accomplished, 'It is enough: the will of GOD will be fulfilled. What can we do?'

True, most true. The will of GOD will be fulfilled. Its execution does not depend upon our v.　endeavour.　But O the difference for each one of us, if we behold it, if we enter into it, if, in our poor measure, we make it our own, if we offer ourselves without reserve for its service.　　　And it is for this reason, we must believe, we are allowed to discern a little of its course.　For the noblest truths are not given us for an intellectual luxury, still less for a moral opiate or a spiritual charm.　They are for the inspiration of our whole being, for the hallowing and for the bracing of every power outward and inward with which we are endowed, for use in the busy fields of common duty.

　　Truth, in a word, cannot remain as a possession of one part of our nature.　If the deed is precious for the sake of the thought of which it is the fruit, the thought must vindicate its power by the corresponding deed.　Man, as he is, is not fully revealed till thought is embodied in deed. And when Descartes had said 'I think, therefore I am,' I cannot but rejoice that our own Whichcote silently corrected the famous sentence by the more memorable phrase ' I act, therefore I am.'

　　And so the greatest of all truths, the truth of the Incarnation, reaches to the innermost recesses of the single life, that it may rouse and guide and sustain him who has welcomed it.　It is, as we have seen, a revelation of love, of sin, of attainment, of sympathy: and it is all this to the individual soul. It is a revelation of humility, of suffering, of faith, issuing in exceeding glory, and it is all this to the solitary believer, self-surrendered, cast down, straining in unwearied effort towards the end which will not disappoint.

St John sets this reflection before us in the Introduction to his Gospel with sublime simplicity. We can hardly miss it if we follow only his main statements, and pass over the parenthetic illustrations with which he explains and enforces them:

In the beginning, we read, *was the Word and the Word was with GOD and the Word was GOD.* John i. 1, 14, 16.

And the Word became flesh and dwelt among us full of grace and truth.

Because out of His fulness all we received and grace for grace.

The Evangelist passes, we see, without one break from the contemplation of the eternal Majesty of GOD to the common experience of his fellow Christians. They all had, he assumes, direct personal knowledge of the power of Christ, answering to His Nature, no less than Apostles who had beheld His glory. The Word, as he teaches, finds a place naturally on the throne of the Father and in the heart of man.

Out of His fulness all we received and grace for John i. 16.

v. · *grace.* The words express two main thoughts. The absolute perfection of all divine power and grace as it can be expressed through humanity is in Christ; in that fact lies the assurance of faith.   And, again, the believer draws from Christ, as from an inexhaustible source, so much vital force as former effort has made him able to use: in that fact lies the law of the activity of faith.   All that any man ever can be is already realised in the Son of man: each man as he puts to use one gift grows capable of receiving a greater.

These thoughts, full of encouragement and of warning, find a typical foreshadowing in a beautiful Jewish legend. It is said that when the Lord spoke from Sinai the voice was heard by the people as they turned this way and that, from North and South from East and West, from earth and heaven. The voice went forth throughout the world and each nation heard it in their own tongue. But they who heard heard it according to their capacity; old men and youths and boys and sucklings and women; and the voice was to each one as each one had power to receive it.

So men pictured to themselves the giving of the Law; and when the Word was manifested that which they had thus fancied became reality. From all sides, in every heart of man, His Message

which is Himself found, as it still finds, expres-   v.
sion and welcome according to the power of love.

Out of His fulness all we received. The perfect assurance of faith rests, I say, in this conviction. In Christ the Word Incarnate, the
divine, the eternal, shines through the forms of
earth unclouded and undimmed.   If there
were found in Him one trait which belonged to some
transitory phase of human growth, to a sect, a
class, a nation, an age, if there were wanting in
Him one characteristic which belongs to the
essence of humanity; one virtue which is the
peculiar glory of man or woman ; we might then
look for another to fulfil the higher type which we   Matt. xi. 3.
should be able to imagine. But, as it is, there
is nothing which we can remove from His
portraiture, nothing which we can add to it, without marring the ideal in which each soul can find
the satisfaction of every desire that it would lay
open in the light of heaven.   We believe
—it is a belief to ponder—that our highest conceivable has been realised by *the Word become
flesh* under the conditions of earth. We believe
not that one man by the cultivation of natural
powers has striven upwards to fellowship with
GOD, but that the Son of GOD has taken humanity
to Himself and gained that for the race which
each member can find for himself in Him. We

v.   believe that that Life of Jesus of Nazareth
matured in silent obscurity and closed in open
shame, that life gladdened only by the joys which
are open to the least of the children of men, the
glories of the sky and field, and the response of
loyal hearts, is the life in which our destiny has
been reached once for all.   We believe
this, and in our impatient strugglings, in our
grasping at shadows, in our sad murmurings, the
belief seems to be on the point of vanishing; but
if it vanishes for a time it is only to reappear in
the darkness, like stars in the night to witness of
other worlds when the sun has set.

    The belief—the belief in the divine fulness of
Christ—is indeed one which it is not easy to keep
in the freshness of its energy.   The ideal which
it proposes is ever escaping from us under the
pressure of sordid cares and fears.   But we gain
no relief from labour by lowering our standard.
We do not rid ourselves of enigmas by abridging
our hopes.   We cast away the Faith;
and what then? The sufferings of earth remain,
but they are emptied of their redemptive potency.
The questionings of partial knowledge remain,
but no response comes with a Gospel of grace and
truth. The mysteries of the finite remain, but
they are not lightened by the assurance that the
human conceptions by which we live as to things

of sense may be trusted no less as to things un-   v.
seen.

Not one difficulty, one pain, one contradiction of
life is removed by the spirit of denial. Only the
treasury of heaven is closed at its bidding ; and
we are charged to stand resigned with our faces
turned towards an impenetrable gloom, through
which the Christian sees a pathway of light, even
the glorified humanity of Christ, leading to the Hebr. x.
throne of GOD.   19 f.

Out of His fulness we all received : 'out of His
fulness :' not from ourselves though in ourselves is
the spring of strength. For Christ's gift, as it
has free course, must stir us with the impulse of a
great devotion. Conscious of our own sins and of our
own forgiveness we shall have learnt to see the
world in a new light. Touched by the love of
Christ we shall feel love. Compassion will gain
for us again its true meaning. We shall minister
to the weak and the erring not in condescend-
ing pity but as enabled to share evils which
are indeed our own.   The power of our
action, as we look to the Son of GOD Incarnate,
will be not fear or sorrow, not even the sense of
right, but reverence for the divine in man.

*Out of His fulness we all received and grace for
grace.* 'Grace for grace :' that is the inexorable
law of the Spirit, the law of the activity of faith.

v.   The higher, nobler, fuller, comes to men only as
the fruit of the lower and the less.

'Light after light well-used they shall attain.'

And in this condition lies for us the promise of
joy growing with growing life.   As each successive
lesson of the Incarnation is learnt, the spirit yet
again takes of that which is Christ's, and shews it *[John xvi. 14.]*
to the believer.   There can be no repetition and
no rest in His teaching.   At the same
time we need to be reminded continually of the
learner's obligation and of the blessing which the
obligation carries.   For of all the perils of advancing age none, as I have said before, is greater
than that of losing the faculty of wonder.   We
become familiar with the sequence of phenomena
and we think that we understand them.   They
move us no longer with the surprise of freshness.
But for the thoughtful the increase of such
knowledge as we can gain adds to the mysteries
of life.   That which is commonest is
indeed the most real cause for wonder.   In this
sense the materials of wonder are continually
gathered about us.   And when the Lord said to
the Jews who were perplexed by His works and
His claims *greater works than these will* [the *[John v. 20.]*
Father] *shew* [the Son], *that ye may marvel*, He
declared the manner of His revelation.   From age

to age He offers to us *grace for grace.* He dis-   v.
closes in the ordinary conditions of life to those
who *have their senses exercised by use* 'greater   Hebr. v.
works' than their fathers saw, more far-reaching   14.
connexions, subtler harmonies, deeper beauties of
life, 'that they may marvel' not in idle astonish-
ment or in vacant curiosity, but as looking beyond
the signs to the spiritual forces which they
suggest.

Yes: that is one of the main lessons of the
Incarnation. It is ever leading us through the
seen to the unseen, offering in this way *grace for
grace;* and so it is that Christianity in consideration of our natures is essentially Sacramental.
So it is that GOD is pleased to take the outward
as the channel of His working: that He uses the
commonest things for the highest ends: that He
binds together the material and the spiritual, in a
union of life: even in order that we may extend
the revelation to all parts of the order in which we
are placed, that we may feel that we are at every
point in contact with unseen powers, that reverence may rest wherever knowledge enters.

At the same time this revelation of the
spiritual grandeur of all life enhances the importance of the single life. Each single life is seen
in the Incarnation to be in the divine plan an
element in the Body of Christ; and we come

v. 　 to understand, when we meditate on the dependences of things, how in the vast chorus of Creation
one voice of 'little human praise' is missed.

And not only does each life gain this solemn
significance from its relation to the vaster life in
which it is included, but each least part of the
individual life assumes a proportionate value.
Nothing can be of the man only: nothing can
be of the body only. The deed of the member,
of the member of the society, of the member of
the family, reaches as far as the life reaches, even
if we have at present no powers to measure its
effects.

This conviction of the illimitable consequences
of action would be of overwhelming awfulness if
we were not able to lift our eyes when the burden
is heaviest to the Son of man; if we were not
able to bring to Him the stained and fragmentary
offering of ourselves and to find in Him that
which is needed to cleanse and to complete it. We
look back indeed for a moment upon the long line
John iv.38. of witnesses whose works, on which we have entered,
attest the efficacy of His unfailing Presence, but
Heb. xii. then we *look away* from all else (ἀφορῶντες) *to*
2. *Jesus the leader and perfecter of faith,* Who in His
humanity met every temptation which can assail
us and crowned with sovereign victory the force
which He offers for our support.

By such experience, such efforts, such reflec-
tions we learn in the stress of life, *receiving grace
for grace,* that the Incarnation is more than an
event: that it is a Truth. We learn that it is a
fact not in the sense that it is past but that it is
eternal. We learn that the fulfilment of
the Incarnation in time is the revelation of that
which is beyond time: the absolute, may we not
say the necessary, seal to us men of the certainty
of the ideas which we are led to fashion under
human conditions of the righteousness and love
of GOD, of the grandeur of the heritage for which
we were born, of the melancholy sentence of
failure which is written against us, of the hope
which we cannot forego that we shall yet see
GOD—see GOD and live.

We meditate on these conclusions; and while
we do so we recognise that the Incarnation reconciles the last terms of that contradiction in life
to which our greatest poets and some of the most
influential teachers of the time bear witness.
For in our noblest literature we find on the one
side a stern and pitiless description of dominant
evil and sorrow, of duty to be sadly if resolutely
followed, of multitudes who can only be dealt
with by some crushing force: and on the other side
we hear a confident appeal to the instinct of beauty
and goodness, to the triumphs of natural heroism,

v.   to the soul of man which struggles through freedom to the light.   We are met, that is, on the one side by the thought of law without the reality of redemption: and on the other side by the thought of love without the reality of the fall.

There is the contradiction from which Nature opens no escape; but in the Incarnation, as a fact, nay, as *the* fact of human life, the fall and the redemption both find complete expression. In the Incarnation law and love are seen in their final harmony.

Brethren, we have touched upon great mysteries, mysteries to be ' kept and pondered in our hearts.' In dealing with them words and thoughts are alike inadequate. So far as these become definite they tend to limit that which is infinite. But their imperfection is not unavailing if it encourages us to strive by the help of the Holy Spirit—and it is a hard task—to know that the revelation of GOD given to us in the Incarnation is given by a living fact, not in a speculation or in a dogma. Forms of thought change, but this Fact vivifies and transcends all.

As a Fact the Incarnation presents intelligibly before our eyes an aim towards which we can bend every energy of our nature.

As a Fact it supplies a motive which stirs us   v.
to devout exertion with an energy proportioned
to the faith with which we apprehend its essence.

As a Fact it is of infinite meaning and able to
minister all that is needed for the hallowing of
toil and study.

As a Fact it is of infinite power and sufficient
to assure help to the weakest servant of GOD.

As a Fact it shews us how that unity to which
physics and history point is not to be found only
in a dispersive connexion of multitudinous parts,
but is summed up finally in One Who is GOD.

As a Fact it supplies a solid foundation for the
loftiest aspirations which man ever fashioned for
himself in the personal consciousness of unsatisfied
longings.

As a Fact, an eternal Fact, realised in time,
may we receive it, hold it, reflect upon it. So
shall we know day by day a little more what it
involves, what it promises, what it enforces, what
it inspires. So shall we draw strength and wisdom
from the very speculations which at first sight
appear to be fraught with danger. So shall we do
the part to which we are called in the building up
of the Church. So shall we offer our little lives,
marred and broken as they are, to Him Who is
able to bring them into fellowship with Himself. Let us hear once again the Gospel

v.   on which we have been allowed to meditate.   *In
the beginning was the Word, and the Word was
with GOD, and the Word was GOD...And the Word
became flesh and dwelt among us...full of grace
and truth...because out of His fulness we all
received, and grace for grace.*

APPENDIX.

THE VISION OF GOD THE CALL OF THE PROPHET.

*Holy, holy, holy, is the Lord of hosts: the whole earth is
full of His glory.*

Is. VI. 3.

TWO years ago it was my duty to speak here as on this day; and now, when I am unexpectedly called to fulfil the same office, my thoughts necessarily go back to the words of the angelic hymn on which I dwelt then. In some form or other the feelings which they express must fill all our hearts. As often as the Festival of the Holy Trinity—the Festival of Revelation—comes round, we are encouraged to lift up our eyes to the manifestation of the divine glory. And through this reverent effort we learn with growing assurance that the contemplation of the majesty of GOD is the source of the largest hope for all His creatures. We come to understand how for beings pure and holy that vision is the call to unfaltering adoration and limitless faith; how for men " of unclean lips," sin-stained and labouring in a sin-stained world, it is the call, the reassuring call, to the prophet's work.

This, then, is the thought which I wish to

APPENDIX. welcome for myself from the services of the day.
This is the thought which I wish to commend to
those who hear me : that the vision of GOD is the
call of the prophet ; that the vision of GOD given
to us to-day in the Triune Name is our call, our
message, our chastening.

1.   The vision of GOD is, I say, the call of the
prophet.   Nowhere is the thought presented to
us in the Bible with more moving force than in
Is. vi. 1–10. the record of Isaiah's mission which we heard
again this morning.   The very mark of time by
which the history is introduced has a pathetic
significance.   It places together in sharp contrast
the hasty presumption of man and the unchanging
love of GOD.   The prophet was called in the year
2 Chron.   that King Uzziah died.   The king died an outcast
xxvi. 16 ff. and a leper because he had ventured to take to
himself the function of a priest in the house of
GOD; and in close connexion with that tragic
catastrophe an access to GOD, far closer than that
which the successful monarch had prematurely
claimed, was foreshewn to the prophet in a
heavenly figure.   Isaiah, a layman, as you remember, was, it appears, in the temple court, and
he saw in a trance the way into the holiest place
laid open.   The veils were removed from sanctuary
and shrine, and he beheld more than met the
Lev. xvi.   eyes of the high priest, the one representative of
the people, on the one day on which he was

admitted year by year to the dark chamber which shrouded the divine presence. He beheld not the glory resting upon the symbolic ark, but the Lord sitting upon the throne high and lifted up; not the carved figures of angels, but the seraphim standing with outstretched wings, ready for swift service; not the vapour of earthly incense, but the cloud of smoke which witnessed to the Majesty which it hid. This opening of "the eyes of his heart" was GOD'S gift, GOD'S call to him. Other worshippers about the young prophet saw, as we must suppose, nothing but "the light of common day," the ordinary sights of the habitual service, the great sea of brass, and the altar of burnt-offering, and the stately portal of the holy place, and Priests and Levites busy with their familiar work. But for an eternal moment Isaiah's senses were unsealed. He saw that which is and not that which appears. For him the symbol of GOD dwelling in light unapproachable, was transformed into a personal presence; for him the chequered scene of human labour and worship was filled with the train of GOD; for him the marvels of human skill were instinct with the life of GOD. The spot which GOD had chosen was disclosed to his gaze as the centre of the divine revelation; but at the same time he was taught to acknowledge that the Divine Presence is not limited by any bounds or excluded by any blindness, when

APPENDIX.
Is. vi. 3.
he heard from the lips of angels that the fulness
of the whole earth is His glory.

Now when we recall what Judaism was at the
time, local, rigid, exclusive, we can at once understand that such a vision, such a revelation taken
into the soul, was for Isaiah an illumination of the
world. He could at last see all creation in its
true nature through the light of GOD. So to have
looked upon it was to have gained that which the
seer, cleansed by the sacred fire, was constrained
to declare. Humbled, and purified in his humilia-
tion, he could have but one answer when the
voice of the Lord required a messenger, "Here am
I: send me."

And as it was then it is now. If that
response of Isaiah seems to us, as it must do, to
be natural or even necessary when we realise his
position, let us not shrink from the confession
that Isaiah's vision, Isaiah's call, are for us also,
and that they await from us a like response.
When the prophet Isaiah looked upon that
John xii.
41.
august sight he saw, as St John tells us, Christ's
glory; he saw in figures and far off that which
we have been allowed to contemplate more nearly
and with the power of closer apprehension. He
saw in transitory shadows that which we have
received in a historic Presence. By the Incarnation GOD has entered, and empowered us to feel
that He has entered, into fellowship with humanity

and men. As often as that truth rises before our APPENDIX.
eyes, all heaven is indeed rent open, and all earth
is displayed as GOD made it. For us, then, the
vision and the call of Isaiah find a fuller form, a
more sovereign voice in the Gospel than the
Jewish prophet could know. And I will dare to
believe that there is not one among us who has
not been quickened to see here, in this home of
generous enthusiasm, glimpses of the prophet's
vision, when he has pondered in some quiet space
of thought the need of the prophet's work in
England or in India; to see disclosed before him
the inner sanctuary of Truth and Love; to see on
the Father's throne, high and lifted up, the Lord
who has lived and died and risen again for him;
to see the folds of His imperial vesture spread
over the whole world, which is His dwelling-place;
to see innumerable hosts of ministering spirits
fulfilling His word in the wide realm of nature;
to see the signs of His Presence, half-splendour
and half-cloud, made known through all the works
of men; to see messengers sent "with live coals
from off the altar" to purify and to kindle those
who shall bear the Gospel to the nations.

Brethren, if, as I believe, you have seen this,
dimly, it may be, and but for a brief moment, and
you above all before whom the work of life is
opening with the fresh fulness of promise in the
purpose of GOD'S grace, be sure that there is

APPENDIX. nothing in life more real than such a vision. It
is the pure light of heaven so broken by the
shadows of earth that we can bear it. Do not
then turn from it, or dismiss it as a dream. Meet
it with the response of glad devotion. It is easy,
alas, to question the authority of the greatest
thoughts which GOD sends to us. It is easy to
darken them and to lose them. But it is not
easy to live on to the end without them. There
is, happily, a noble discontent which disturbs all
self-centred pleasure. And, on the other hand,
you must have been allowed to feel that you are
stirred with the truest joy, and braced to labour
best at your little tasks, while you welcome and
keep before you the loftiest ideal of the method
and the aim of work and being which GOD has
made known to you. That is, indeed, His revelation, the vision of Himself. So He declares what
He would have you to do, what He will enable
you to do. So He calls you to be prophets.

Yes: for us the vision of GOD, the vision of
this day is a prophet's call. And let us gratefully
recognise the divine order in which it is presented
to us. The Festival of Revelation follows the
Festival of the Spirit. The Festival of the Spirit
closes the cycle of the historic festivals of the
Church. And now all the facts of the historic
Gospel are crowned by the thought of GOD in
Himself; and that thought, summed up in the

Triune Name into which we were baptised, is APPENDIX.
offered to us afresh to-day for calm study. We
are called upon to use the "power from on high Luke xxiv.
with which we have been clothed," to regard yet ^{49.}
once again with questioning devotion the secret
of the eternal life which has been made known to
us for the use of earth in the Person of Christ.

And what, therefore, we ask, does *the mys-
tery*, the revelation *of GOD, even Christ,* mean for Col. ii. 2.
us, the mystery of which we are ministers and
prophets, the mystery which brings the eternal
within the forms of time, the mystery which shews
to us absolute love made visible in the Incarnate
Word ? It means—it must mean if only we
think patiently and calmly—that the outward,
the transitory, is a veil woven by the necessities
of our weakness which half hides and half reveals
the realities with which it corresponds ; it means
that the changing forms in which spiritual aspirations are clothed from generation to generation
and from life to life, are illuminated, quickened,
harmonised in one supreme fact ; it means that
beyond the temples in which it is our blessing to
worship and beyond the phrases which it is our
joy to affirm, there is an infinite glory which can
have no local circumscription, and an infinite
Truth which cannot be grasped by any human
thought ; it means that man, bruised and burdened by sorrows and sins, was made for GOD, and

APPENDIX. that through His holy love he shall not fail of his destiny ; it means that all creation is an expression of GOD'S thought of wisdom brought within John xiv. 26. the reach of human intelligence ; it means that GOD'S Spirit sent in His Son's name will interpret little by little, as we can read the lesson, all things as contributory to His praise ; it means that we also, compassed with infirmities and burdened with sins, may take up the song of the redeemed creation, the song of the unfallen angels, and say, "Holy, holy, holy, is the Lord of hosts : the fulness of the earth is His glory." It means this, and more than this, more than mind can shape and tongue can utter, and, as the light streams in upon us, we cannot refuse to acknowledge the obligation by which we are bound to make known that which is made plain by its brightness ; to interpret to others according to the teaching of our own experience the truth which has been disclosed to our souls.

2.   For even as the vision of GOD is the call of the prophet, so it is this vision which the prophet has to proclaim and to interpret to his fellow-men, not as an intellectual theory, but as an inspiration of life. The prophet's teaching must be the translation of his experience. He bears witness of that which he has seen. His words are not an echo but a living testimony. The heart alone can speak to the heart. But he

who has beheld the least fragment of the divine APPENDIX.
glory, he who has spelt out in letters of light on
the face of the world one syllable of the Triune
Name, will have a confidence and a power which
nothing else can bring. Only let him trust what
he has seen, and it will become to him a guid-
ing-star till he rests in the unveiled Presence of
Christ.

And so let us all thank GOD, on this Festival
of Revelation, that He has called us in the fulfilment of our prophet's office to unfold a growing
message and not to rehearse a stereotyped tradition. The Gospel of Christ Incarnate, the Gospel
of the Holy Trinity in the terms of human life,
which we have to announce, covers every imagin-
able fact of life to the end of time, and is new
now as it has been new in all the past, as it will
be new, new in its power and new in its meaning,
while the world lasts. It was new when St John
at Ephesus was enabled to express its fundamental
truth in the doctrine of the Word; new when
Athanasius at Nicæa affirmed through it the
living unity of the Godhead without derogating
from the Lord's Deity; new when Anselm at Bec
sought in it, however partially and inadequately,
a solution of the problem of eternal justice; new
when Luther at Wittenberg found in it the ground
of personal communion with GOD; new in our
own generation, new with an untold message,

APPENDIX. when we are bidden to acknowledge in it the pledge of that ultimate fellowship of created things which the latest researches in nature and in history offer for consecration.

For this supreme unity, which is neither monotonous nor barren, and nothing less than this, answers, as I have already indicated, to that vision of GOD in Christ, "the true GOD," "the GOD of hope," which is presented to this age. And we therefore, as we behold the Divine Image under the light of our own day, must labour to bring to our view of "the world"—the order for a time separated from GOD—that thought of GOD which makes it again a fit object of our love as it is the object of the love of GOD: to bring to our view of society that conviction of dependence and connexion which is at once a safeguard and a motive force: to bring to our view of the present that sense of eternity which transfigures our estimate of great and small, of success and failure.

The transformation of life requires no more: it is possible with no less. And to us as Christians the charge is given to bear this prophetic message to men.

True it is that such a vision of GOD—Creator, Redeemer, Sanctifier—entering into fellowship with the beings whom He has made, "reconciling all things unto Himself, having made peace through the blood of the Cross," shews life to us, as

John xvii. 3. Rom. xv. 13.

John iii. 16.

Col. i. 20.

Isaiah saw it, in a most solemn aspect: that it APPENDIX. must fill us, as it filled Isaiah, with the sense of our immeasurable unworthiness in the face of Christ's majesty and Christ's love: that it must touch us also with something of a cleansing power. And because it is so we can take heart again.

For such emotion, such purification of soul, is the beginning of abiding strength. "He that wonders shall reign"—"He that is near me is near fire"—are among the few traditional sayings attributed to the Lord which seem to be stamped as divine. Awe, awe the lowliest and the most self-suppressing, is a sign not of littleness, but of nobility. Our power of reverence is a measure of our power of rising. As we bow in intelligent worship before the face of our King, His Spirit— a Spirit of fire—enters into us. We feel that we are made partakers of the Divine nature because we can acknowledge with a true faith its spiritual glories, and lay ourselves

> Passive and still before the awful Throne . . .
> Consumed, yet quickened, by the glance of GOD.

3. So we come to the last consideration which I desire to suggest. The vision of GOD is, as we have seen, the call of the prophet, and the message of the prophet. It is also the chastening of the prophet.

And in the fulfilment of our prophetic work

we need, I think, more than we know the abasing
and elevating influences which the vision of
Isaiah and the thoughts of to-day are fitted to
create or deepen. In the stress of restless occu-
pation we are tempted to leave too much out of
sight the inevitable mysteries of life. We deal
lightly with the greatest questions. We are
peremptory in defining details of dogma beyond
the teaching of Scripture. We are familiar
beyond apostolic precedent in our approaches to
GOD. We fashion heavenly things after the
fashion of earth. We are like Mary Magdalene,
who in her mistaken love would have kept her
John xx. Lord as she had first known Him, when as yet the
17. Ascension had not revealed the nature of an
eternal fellowship, and made such fellowship
possible; and once more Christ, as we recognise
Him at first under the conditions of earth, seems
to be saying to us, "'Cling not to Me,' not with
the hand but with the soul must you hold Me if
you would enjoy My abiding presence."

In all these respects then, for our strengthening and for our purifying, we must seek for ourselves, and strive to spread about us, the sense of
the awfulness of being, as those who have seen
Apoc. iv. GOD at Bethlehem, Calvary, Olivet, and on the
2 f. throne encircled by a rainbow as an emerald: the
sense, vague and imperfect at the best, of the
illimitable range of the courses and issues of

action : the sense of the untold vastness of that APPENDIX. life which we are bold to measure by our feeble powers: the sense of the Majesty of Him before Whom the angels veil their faces. If we are cast down by the meannesses, the sorrows, the sins of the world, it is because we dwell on some little part of which we see little; but let the thought of GOD in Christ come in, and we can rest in that holy splendour. At the same time let us not dare to confine at our will the action of the light. It is our own irreparable loss if in our conceptions of doctrine we gain clearness of definition by following out the human conditions of apprehending the divine, and forget that every outline is the expression in terms of a lower order of that which is many sided; if in our methods of devotion we single out the human nature of the Lord, or rather the manifestation of His unascended manhood, as the object of our thoughts, and forget that He leads us to the Father ; if we rest in things visible and do not rather strive to read ever more clearly the spiritual lessons to which they point; if we concentrate our worship in isolated rites and fail to bear to the world of daily thought and action the teaching and the promises of Sacraments.

Brethren, the thoughts on which we have touched open unfathomable depths of duty. But it is good for us to reflect on the greatness of GOD

APPENDIX. which is as immeasurable as His love. And may He in His great mercy cleanse our dull eyes, and check our hasty tongues, and calm our impetuous reasonings; and so, in the solemn calm, the vision of Him—Father, Son, and Holy Ghost— will take shape slowly before us. So we shall still recognise in it our call, our message, our spirit, as prophets touched by His fire. We shall say with the lowliest confession of our unworthiness, " our eyes have seen the King, the Lord of Hosts." We shall reply with the most absolute self-surrender to the voice which asks in our hearts for messengers to make truth known, each according to our ability: " Here am I : send me." And in the lifelong fulfilment of our work, undismayed by the darkness which we cannot penetrate, undeterred by the weakness which we cannot overcome, we shall repeat the song of heaven, which the Incarnation has fitted for the lips of men, " Holy, holy, holy, is the Lord of hosts, the fulness of the earth is His glory."

ST MARY'S, CAMBRIDGE.
Trinity Sunday, 1885.

CAMBRIDGE : PRINTED AT THE UNIVERSITY PRESS.